On the Eve of Adam

God's Ancient Plan For Lucifer's Defeat

Dr. J. R. Church

All Scripture references are from the King James Version of the Bible unless otherwise stated.

On the Eve of Adam
God's Ancient Plan for Lucifer's Defeat
First Edition, 2001
Copyright © 2001 by Prophecy in the News, Inc.

Printed in the United States of America

Published by:
Prophecy Publications
P. O. Box 7000
Oklahoma City, OK 73153

Library of Congress Control Number: 2001 130823
ISBN 0-941241-21-1

To my dear wife and companion through life,
Linda

Foreword

The stories in the Bible are true. They are not fables concocted around the campfires of ancient cavemen. The writings of Moses give an accurate historical account of the early history of the human race. The stories of Adam and his progeny may not be exhaustive, but are sufficient, from heaven's viewpoint, to give us a pattern for God's ancient plan, devised on the eve of Adam — before his creation — for the defeat of Lucifer.

One may wonder why we are not given at least a thousand pages of details on the 930 years Adam lived. Where did he reside? What did he do? How many children did he and Eve bring into this world? What were their names? These are details left out of the biblical narrative. But what is given, is enough for God to lay out a prophetic pattern to be fulfilled by the future second Adam — the *"seed"* of Eve. His mission was *"to reconcile all things unto himself ... whether they be things in earth, or things in heaven"* (Col. 1:20).

This book is by no means exhaustive. There are so many types and symbols that allude to God's plan of the ages, several volumes would be needed to even begin to expound upon them. But the types and symbols that are expounded in this book will inspire and guide its readers to uncover new areas in the grand design of our Lord, for the redemption of all who believe and the subsequent defeat and judgment of Lucifer.

Table of Contents

Chapter One

God's Plan of the Ages

Adam was not an afterthought. Contrary to popular opinion, God did not create man because He was lonely. Furthermore, Adam's transgression was not the original sin. Lucifer's rebellion preceded the events of Eden.

was he serpent n heaven?

Heaven must have been in turmoil after the fall of the serpent; a third of the angels were affected. Some wonder why God didn't just evaporate His foe and be done with it. Why does Lucifer continue to operate to this very day? He has created so much heartache and chaos. He has spoiled everything he touches. Why does God continue to put up with him?

Rest assured that God has a plan. He formulated it somewhere in the ancient past, prior to the creation of Adam. There was a divine reason why God has allowed Lucifer to follow through with his diabolical scheme. In the end, God will restore tranquility to His kingdom. And to do so, God laid out a strategy for complete and total victory. It involved the creation of the human race, knowing all the while that Adam would fall for Lucifer's lies.

God's plan was not formulated as the events of history unfolded. Every detail was carefully organized before the creation of Adam. In order to convince us that He was in complete control, God had His ancient plan written into the stories of the Old Testament. Furthermore, the Creator assured us that His plan was preordained:

*"Remember the former things of old: for **I am God**, and there is none else; I am God, and there is none like me,*

*"**Declaring the end from the beginning**, and from ancient times the things that are not yet done..."* (Isaiah 46:9,10).

Declaring the End

God did not wait until the days of Moses before formulating His plan. Nor did He lay it out in the days of Abraham. Furthermore, God was not frustrated over man's rebellion in the days of Noah. God declared His prophetic plan to the pair in the Garden. Furthermore, God's plan was not concluded at Calvary. The verse does not say that God declared the "middle" from the beginning. He declared the *"end."* Since mankind is still filling this planet with people, it is obvious that God's plan is not yet over.

According to the sages of Israel, God delivered His prophetic plan of the ages through the six days of Creation. Those six days represent six thousand years.

The seventh day, upon which God rested, lays out a prophetic plan in which the seventh millennium will be ushered in as a "great Sabbath rest." Utopia will soon come to this planet. It is a part of God's plan for Lucifer's defeat.

Heaven Is Included in the Plan

Many Christians think that the crucifixion of Christ was intended only for the redemption of the human race. But the Bible indicates that redemption is only part of the plan. Christ went to the cross that He might bring about a spiritual reconciliation of heaven as well. Paul alludes to this concept in his letter to the Colossians:

"And, having made peace through the blood of his cross, by him to reconcile all things unto himself; by him, I say, whether they be things in earth, or things in heaven" (Colossians 1:20).

We do not know the whole story, but the reconciliation of heaven seems to be very much a part of the Calvary experience. Perhaps we are not the only ones who benefited from the sacrifice of our Savior.

We are all familiar with John 3:16, but are you aware that the Greek term for *"world"* is cosmos? When John penned, *"For God so loved the **world**,"* he did not use the term for earth. He used the Greek word *cosmos,* meaning *"the heavens and the earth"* — a term that includes both this existence and the heavenly realm. The *Zondervan Pictoral Encyclopedia of the Bible* (vol. 1, page 982) notes that the plural "heavens" also includes "… the place of God's residence." Consider what the Bible says about the ongoing spiritual war between God and the devil. This conflict started before the making of Adam and continues throughout history. The story of the devil's defeat is intricately connected to the events of the end time. The fall of the old dragon is the primary theme of the book of Revelation.

We are not told simply that believers will be saved and that unbelievers will be condemned. There is another factor presented in the story of the final judgment — the devil will be defeated. Don't forget this all-important aspect of redemption's story.

Every war, every crime, and every atrocity befalling mankind was hatched in hell. The human race faces a common enemy. Lucifer's plot is behind every rebellion. His plan is simple — divide and conquer. He is determined to thwart the will of God.

Whenever there is a war on the earth, there appears to be a coinciding conflict in the spirit realm. An example of this extra-dimensional warfare is given in the book of Daniel. An angel was dispatched as soon as Daniel began to pray. However, it took twenty-one days before he finally reached the prophet:

"Then said he unto me, Fear not, Daniel: for from the first day that thou didst set thine heart to understand, and to chasten thyself before thy God, thy words were heard, and I am come for thy words.

"But the prince of the kingdom of Persia withstood me one and twenty days: but, lo, Michael, one of the chief princes, came to help me; and I remained there with the kings of Persia" (Daniel 10:12,13).

There is no human potentate that could stop an angel for three weeks. It is assumed, therefore, that this *"prince"* is a demonic creature with diabolical authority within the kingdom of Persia. By the way, he is probably still there. Daniel, an advisor to the king of Persia, was made aware of this unseen force at work in the political hierarchy of the land. The battle plan originates in the spirit realm, but the earth has become the battlefield.

Battlefield Earth

Consider the possibility that our universe was originally made for Lucifer's domain. The Apostle Paul called him *"the god of this world"* (II Corinthians 4:4). It seems that he was the leader of a serpentine group of creatures. For that reason, he is referred to as a *"serpent"* and *"dragon"* throughout the Bible. Fossils of his subjects are found all over the world. Archeologists have coined the term "dinosaur" from the Greek (δεινοσ) "terrifying" and (σαυροσ) "lizards" to explain their appearance. We know very little about these followers of Lucifer, only that they actually existed somewhere in ages past and suffered a dramatic extinction.

Furthermore, scientists have examined photographs of the planets and moons in our solar neighborhood and noted catastrophic damage. In fact, the entire universe appears to be cursed by the fall of Lucifer. The Creation that God once observed as *"good"* now appears to be dying. We can thank Lucifer for that.

Since this universe is a part of the broken Creation, it was necessary that Jesus bring the battle into this realm. The strategy for the conflict may have been formulated in another dimension, but the battle involves this dimension. In order for the Son of God to bring the battle to earth, He created the human race. Mankind provided a human form whereby the Son of God could be incarnated into this realm.

I do not pretend to know every aspect of God's ancient plan, but I am convinced that it involves more than just the human race. We are not some Divine experiment. We are not mere pawns in a heavenly game of chess. We are vital to God's plan for Lucifer's defeat. Furthermore, it was God's love that caused Him to formulate this seven-thousand-year plan. Had He simply eliminated His foe on the spot, the rest of heaven would never have known about the depths of the rebellion, or the greatness of His victory. It is not a simple story.

The Stouthearted

Isaiah also tells us why God has declared his seven-thousand year plan from the beginning. He wants to convince the staunchest unbeliever that He is fully aware of every situation in life. The *"stouthearted"* must be made to understand that nothing happens by accident. God is in complete control from the very beginning:

"Calling a ravenous bird from the east, the man that executeth my counsel from a far country: yea, I have spoken it, I will also bring it to pass; I have purposed it, I will also do it.

"Hearken unto me, ye stouthearted, that are far from righteousness:
*"I bring near my righteousness; it shall not be far off, and my **salvation** shall not tarry: and I will place salvation in Zion for Israel my glory"* (Isaiah 46:11-13).

The *"ravenous bird from the east"* is descriptive of the end-time battles that begin with Gog and Magog and conclude at Armageddon. Ezekiel 39 tells us that God will use birds to eat the flesh of the slain upon the battlefield.

John also describes the scene for us in Revelation 19. This is a part of the *"end"* in the plan that God declares. And why are we told about it? Because the *"stouthearted that are far from righteousness"* must be made to understand God's ancient plan for Lucifer's defeat. The primary purpose for declaring His ancient plan is so that we might use it as proof for convincing a skeptical mankind. We should use the study of eschatology to reach the lost with the Gospel.

In fact, every person who has ever received Christ has done so in order to settle his or her future destiny. Therefore, prophecy (a view of the future) is at the root of every conversion.

The term *"salvation"* is used twice in Isaiah 46. The Hebrew root in each case spells the ancient name of Jesus. God is saying, *"my Jesus shall not tarry...."* He promises to "place Jesus in Zion...." The passage starts out by saying, *"I am God, and there is none else"* and concludes by naming Jesus as the author of *"salvation."*

Jesus is God in the fullest definition of the term. There should be no doubt as to His Deity. He is the embodiment and the essence of the Godhead. He was willing to identify Himself with man in order to reconcile both the heavens and the earth.

Types and Symbols

In order to explain His ancient plan to the believer while, at the same time, hiding it from the prying eyes of Lucifer, God used types and symbols.

For example, Adam displayed characteristics that allude to the "last Adam," Jesus Christ. Adam identified with his wife and took her sin upon himself in order to insure her salvation. In like manner, Christ took our sin upon Himself and died to pay the price for our redemption.

As Abraham was about to sacrifice his son, he became a type of the heavenly Father, while Isaac's submission to the sacrifice portrayed a type of Christ.

Joseph was rejected and later accepted as the redeemer of his people — an excellent example of the First and Second Advents of Christ.

Ruth was a Gentile bride who married the "kinsman redeemer." She displayed the characteristics of New Testament Christianity.

The Judges displayed God's ancient plan through their exploits.

David, a man after God's own heart, became a type

of Christ, as he was promised that the Lord would come from his lineage.

The wisdom of Solomon became a symbol of Christ, being the scion of the house of David.

Elijah's ministry foreshadowed the events of the end time as Ahab portrays the Antichrist and Jezebel takes the part of Mystery Babylon.

The Old Testament is filled with many such stories, demonstrating that God *"declared the end from the beginning."* As you study these stories from the Old Testament, look for the plan. It is there.

Chapter Two

From Adam to Noah

There are many references to God's ancient plan throughout the New Testament, and though they are plainly stated to be prophetic in nature, they are often overlooked. For example, in writing to the church at Rome, the Apostle Paul referred to Adam as a prophetic figure of Christ:

"Nevertheless death reigned from Adam to Moses, even over them that had not sinned after the similitude of Adam's transgression, who is the figure of him that was to come" (Romans 5:14).

In I Corinthians 15, Paul referred to Christ as the last Adam:

"The first man Adam was made a living soul; the last Adam was made a quickening spirit.
"The first man is of the earth, earthy: the second man is the Lord from heaven" (I Corinthians 15:45,47).

It stands to reason that God would begin immediately after the fall of Adam to present His prophetic plan of the ages to the earliest civilization. God did not wait until the days of Moses to begin laying out His prophetic pattern. He began with Adam — and from the life of that first human being, God revealed His plan for the 7,000 year history of man.

In Adam's case, God used a series of contrasts in order to make him a figure of Christ who was to come and fulfill the prophetic profile. For instance, Paul wrote:

"For as in Adam all die, even so in Christ shall all be made alive" (I Corinthians 15:22).

Death came by Adam, but eternal life comes by Jesus Christ. Through Adam came eternal judgment, but through Christ will come eternal blessing.

Adam was given dominion over the beast of the field, the fowl of the air, and over all the earth. Yet, through sin, he lost his title to the inheritance. On the other hand, Christ will come to rule and reign as King of kings and Lord of lords. Though Adam yielded to the temptations of Satan, Jesus did not.

Eve

Since Adam is a prophetic figure of Jesus Christ, then Eve, his bride, must be a type of New Testament Christianity — the bride of Christ. Adam gave life to Eve. In like manner, Christ gave eternal life to us. As Eve was taken from the side of Adam, New Testament Christianity has been taken from the riven side of Christ:

"But He was wounded for our transgressions, he was bruised for our iniquities: the chastisement of our peace was upon him; and with his stripes we are healed" (Isaiah 53:5). According to the Scriptures, Eve was deceived in the fall, yet Adam was not. Adam was willing to take her sin upon himself. The sin of Eve was accounted to Adam. He was willing to become identified with her sin. In like manner, Jesus took our sin upon Himself, that He might become our substitute, and suffer our consequences.

Eve also represented a series of contrasts. For example, though Eve was deceived, New Testament Christianity has been enlightened and has partaken of the Tree of Life. Just as Eve was clothed with the *shekinah* glory and lost it, New Testament Christianity was clothed with *shekinah* glory (on the Day of Pentecost) and cannot lose it. The life possessed by Adam and Eve was temporary. In contrast to that, however, the life possessed by Christ and His Church is eternal.

Finally, Eve, as a type of New Testament Christianity, bore children to her husband. It is likewise the responsibility of Christians to win people to Christ — to birth them into the family of God — to bring men to the place where they might be *"born again."*

Abel, Cain, and Seth

Eve bore three sons to Adam which are of particular significance. First, there was Cain. He appears to be a type of apostate religion. When Cain brought his offering before the Lord, it was a bloodless sacrifice — the works of his own hands. Cain was typical of that kind of religious zeal that killed the saints and brought on the Dark Ages.

On the other hand, Eve brought forth a second son named Abel. He appears to be a type of faithful Christianity. Abel was a fundamentalist. When he brought his offering before the Lord, it was a blood sacrifice, just as God had prescribed. Abel believed in salvation by substitution. He practiced salvation by grace while Cain believed in salvation by works.

Fortunately, however, the typology does not end with the death of Abel. Eve brought forth yet a third son and called him Seth. The name comes from an ancient Hebrew term meaning "restitution." Seth is reminiscent of the Reformation. The reformers of Christianity during the 16th century, brought a breath of fresh air to Christian theology, pulled the world out of the Dark Ages, and set in motion a return to biblical Christianity.

But that's not all. Seth bore a son named Enos; Enos bore a son named Cainan; Cainan bore a son named Mahalaleel; Mahalaleel bore a son named Jared; Jared bore a son named Enoch; Enoch bore a son named Methuselah; Methuselah bore a son named

Lamech; and Lamech bore a son named Noah. Each of these men, in their own right, present an uncanny prophetic parallel to a projected 7,000 years of human history.

The first six men among those ten seem to represent 6,000 years of history. The next four, Enoch, Methuselah, Lamech, and Noah, seem to represent those events which will attend the end of the sixth millennium, and introduce the seventh.

Adam - The First Millennium

Let us begin by considering the first six generations. There was Adam, Seth, Enos, Cainan, Mahalaleel, and Jared. Each of these men lived almost a thousand years. Furthermore, each seems to represent six separate and successive millennia.

God had said to Adam:

*"In the **day** that thou eatest thereof thou shalt surely die"* (Genesis 2:17).

That *"day"* sets the theme for a millennium — 1,000 years. Adam died after living 930 years. He missed living that 1,000 year *"day"* by a period of 70 years. It is quite remarkable that the lifespan of man has been set at threescore and ten. It is our lot to live those 70 years that Adam was not allowed to live.

Peter wrote that *"one day is with the Lord as a thousand years, and a thousand years as one day"* (II Peter 3:8). In light of that basic rule of interpretation, the warning made to Adam becomes clear. Adam died near the end of the first millennial *"day"* in which he ate the forbidden fruit.

Therefore, Adam represented the first millennium of human history, and each succeeding generation after him represented another millennium. In the lives of those first six men, we may view a magnificent prophetic picture of 6,000 years of human history.

The name Adam has two possible meanings. In Hebrew, if the word Adam is used as a noun, it means "ground" but if used as a verb, it means "red, ruddy, flush" or "red in the face." It bears the connotation of a blush and reveals guilt. Such was the human race in the first millennium — guilty!

"Wherefore, as by one man sin entered into the world, and death by sin; and so death passed upon all men, for that all have sinned" (Romans 5:12).

Seth - The Second Millennium

The second millennium of history appears to be depicted through the life of Seth. The name Seth comes from an ancient Hebrew word meaning "restitution" or "substituted." It is descriptive of the second millennium wherein the human race was destroyed by the Flood and Noah's family was chosen to bring forth a substitute human race. Seth also means "to appoint." In like manner, Noah was appointed by God to bring restitution to God's condemned Creation.

Enos - The Third Millennium

The third generation, Enos, son of Seth, appears to be indicative of the third millennium. Enos means "another" (it also means "mortal") and alludes to Abraham who was called to leave his family and travel to a land, said God, *"that I will show thee."*

According to the Scriptures, in those days *"men began to call upon the name of the Lord."* What a picture of Abraham! From Abraham came the Chosen People, as was implied in the name Enos, "another." There was Isaac, Jacob, and his twelve sons. To their offspring was given the Promise Land.

Cainan - The Fourth Millennium

The fourth generation appears to be typical of the fourth millennium. The son of Enos was named Cainan. Even his name alludes to the Promised Land.

During the fourth millennium, the Chosen People settled in land with a similar name — Canaan. The name Cainan means "fixed nest." Its meaning implies a home, a place one can call his own. It was a land flowing with milk and honey. Therefore, Cainan is a type of the events of the fourth millennium.

Mahalaleel - The Fifth Millennium

The fifth millennium may be viewed through the name of Cainan's son, Mahalaleel, meaning "praise of God." It was at the beginning of the fifth millennium that Christ was born. From the First Advent of

Christ has come the great praise of God — eternal life for all who believe. Mahalaleel appears to be typical of the fifth millennium which instituted the dispensation of *Grace* and the development of New Testament Christianity.

Jared - The Sixth Millennium

The sixth millennium appears to be represented by Jared, the son of Mahalaleel. Jared means "a descent" and that is exactly what should take place at the end of the sixth millennium when the Savior returns! The two men, Mahalaleel and Jared, appear to represent 2,000 years of Christianity, at the end of which there will be a descent! These first six men appear to represent a brief but important foreview of 6,000 years.

Concluding Events

The collective events which are destined to conclude God's plan of the ages seem to be profiled in the next four men — Enoch, Methuselah, Lamech, and Noah. In them, we may view the Rapture and Resurrection of the saints, the Tribulation Period, and the return of Christ to establish His Millennial Kingdom upon the earth, wherein He shall reign for that seventh 1,000 year period of history.

Enoch - The Rapture

When the typology in Jared is about to be completed, Enoch offers a view of the first important end-time event. Enoch means "dedicated one." Therefore, Enoch is a type of the Rapture, when all dedicated ones will be taken *"in a moment, in the twinkling of an eye"* (I Corinthians 15:52). We are told that *"Enoch walked with God: and he was not; for God took him"* (Genesis 5:24). He was the first human to be raptured alive into heaven and appears to be a profile of that future event when we shall hear the shout and the trumpet sound.

Enoch lived 365 years before he was raptured. That number makes him the "calendar man." Just as there are 365 days in a year, Enoch lived 365 years. I believe those years represent a key which unlocks the mystery in the study of times. There are certain places in prophecy where a day represents one year.

For example, Israel spent 40 years in the wilderness because they refused to believe the spies who spent 40 days in the Promised Land. In His anger, God told Moses that the people would spend a year in the wilderness for each day those men were in the Promised Land.

Daniel's prophecy of the seventy weeks can be understood only when we realize that each week was a prophetic picture of seven years. Each day represented one year. Perhaps Enoch was the key to the understanding of these mysteries.

since these last 4 men are symbolic of 6000 years together, could all these events happen together? Do they need to happen in order where one leads to another?

Methuselah - The Tribulation

[Once the Rapture has taken place, the next man will come into focus.] His name is Methuselah, the son of Enoch. The name Methuselah is said to mean "man of the dart." In the Hebrew language the word refers to a "missile of attack." His name implies violence and wickedness. Such is the description of the Tribulation Period. The definition "missile of attack" may well represent those wars of the last generation — concluding at Armageddon. Methuselah was a man of the javelin. He is thought to have been a wicked man who used the javelin for evil purposes.

Furthermore, the last part of his name, selah (according to the *Zondervan Pictorial Encyclopedia of the Bible*), is a proper name indicating idolatry. Such is the picture of humanity during these closing days of world history. Idolatry abounds on every hand. Violence and wickedness are descriptive of our day.

His name also comes from a Hebrew root meaning "when he is dead, it will come." Please note, Methuselah was the oldest man who ever lived. He lived 969 years and seems to prophetically represent the long-suffering of Christ who is not willing that any should perish but that all should come to repentance.

Lamech - The Revelation

With Enoch being a picture of the Rapture and Methuselah a type of the Tribulation Period, let us consider Lamech, son of Methuselah, and father of Noah. According to the *Strong's Exhaustive Concordance of the Bible*, Lamech comes from an ancient unused root whose meaning remains a mystery.

There is something mysterious about Lamech and his prophetic significance. It may represent the "mystery of God" referred to in the New Testament. An example of this is given in Revelation 10:

"But in the days of the voice of the seventh angel, when he shall begin to sound, the **mystery** *of God should be finished, as he hath declared to his servants the prophets"* (Rev. 10:7).

This *"mystery"* has essentially remained unanswered throughout history. However, one day that mystery will be revealed. Lamech seems to be a prophetic picture of that event. We have two clues, however, which may be of some help. According to the *Zondervan Pictorial Encyclopedia of the Bible*, there is a suggestion that his name may mean "strong man." That is clue number one. Our second clue is that he lived 777 years.

It is possible that Lamech represents the Second Coming of Christ. First of all, the possible definition, "strong man," is definitely descriptive of our Savior's coming in power and glory to single-handedly conquer the armies of the world.

Second, Lamech lived 777 years. Those three numbers contrast with the number of the Antichrist. Six represents the number of man and seven represents the number of divine completion. It is the number of Deity. The number of that final man of sin is given in Revelation 13:18, as 666. Surely, this 777, covering the life of Lamech, prophetically represents the future "strong man" who will come and win the day.

Furthermore, Lamech produced Noah, whose name means "rest." In like manner, at His return, the Lord Jesus Christ will produce the kingdom, also known as the great "Sabbath Rest."

The Genesis Apocraphon

Among the hundreds of documents found in the caves at Qumran, there was an ancient scroll which has been called *The Genesis Apocraphon*. In the document, Lamech was described as being tired of the unproductive soil. It is said that he expected his son, Noah, to remove the curse of Adam. Noah, being the tenth generation from Adam, represented the fulfillment of the Edenic promise.

The number ten (in the scroll) is said to have a spiritual significance. It represented completion, or conclusion. According to E. W. Bullinger, in his book *"Number in Scripture,"* ten represents the number of "ordinal perfection." Prophetically, Noah (the tenth generation) represents the conclusion of human history and the great Sabbath Rest. No wonder Jesus said in Matthew 24:37, *"But as the days of Noe were, so shall also the coming of the Son of man be."*

Noah - The Kingdom Rest

The life of Noah offers the most spectacular prophetic significance. If Enoch is typical of the saints being raptured before the Tribulation, then Noah, during the Flood, may be a type of Israel who had to endure those seven years.

I realize that Noah was safe from the Flood, being inside the ark. Nevertheless, he had to endure the discomfort of those buffeting waves against the sides of the ship. It must have been a wild ride! In like manner, though the Jewish people will be preserved, they must, nevertheless, endure those years of *"Jacob's trouble."* These men represent a magnificent prophecy. God was declaring the end from the beginning!

Chapter Three

Abraham, Isaac, and Jacob

Many Old Testament biographies offer insights into God's redemptive plan of the ages. The lives of these men present unmistakable profiles that conform to a single, though complex, prophetic pattern.

It seems that God intended for His people to know the future. Therefore, even in those early years of human civilization, God allowed a pattern to emerge from the lives of His Chosen People. Over and over again we can glean prophetic truth from the stories of these ancient heroes. One such story is told in the lives of Abraham, Isaac, and Jacob.

Abraham appears to be a type of God the Father; Isaac, his son, is typical of Jesus Christ; and, in like manner, Jacob, whose name was changed to Israel, appears to be a profile of *Law*, as seen in Jacob, being turned into *Grace*, as seen in Israel.

Let us take a closer look and see what prophecies can be gleaned from the lives of these great men. Our study will center primarily around Isaac who was a prophetic symbol of Jesus Christ. However, in the course of our study, we must take note of the others around him who fit into the overall picture of the prophecy. Keep in mind that these biblical narratives are true and accurate.

Abraham, Hagar, Sarah, and Keturah

First, there was Abraham, the father of the faithful. If he is a type of God the Father then we must account for his three wives; Hagar, Sarah and Keturah.

According to Galatians 4, Hagar was an allegory of the dispensation of *Law*. As such, she would represent the Old Testament religion of Judaism. The Apostle Paul called her a bondmaid:

"For it is written, that Abraham had two sons, the one by a bondmaid, the other by a freewoman.
"But he who was of the bondwoman was born after the flesh; but he of the freewoman was by promise.
*"Which things are an **allegory**: for these are the two covenants; the one from the mount Sinai, which gendereth to bondage, which is Agar"* (Galatians 4:22-24).

According to Paul, Hagar represented the bondage of *Law*. Sarah, on the other hand, was a free woman. That which was born of her represented God's promise. Sarah represents New Testament Christianity. Note verses 30 and 31:

"Nevertheless what saith the scripture? Cast out the bondwoman and her son: for the son of the bondwoman shall not

be heir with the son of the freewoman.
"So then, brethren, we are not children of the bondwoman,
but of the free" (Galatians 4:30-31).

The meaning of the name Hagar is uncertain. However, it may have emerged from an ancient Hebrew root meaning "to remove or to take away." It also refers to "one who murmurs." Well, she certainly seems to fit both definitions.

Sarah

The name Sarah was given to Abraham's wife when she was 90 years old. At that time, God promised her a son and instructed her to call his name Isaac:

*"And God said unto Abraham, As for Sarai thy wife, thou shalt not call her name Sarai, but **Sarah** shall her name be ...*
*"And God said, Sarah thy wife shall bear thee a **son** indeed; and thou shalt call his name **Isaac**: and I will establish my covenant with him for an everlasting covenant, and with his seed after him"* (Genesis 17:15,19).

Sarah's original name, Sarai, meant "to dominate." Once she was given the promise of a son, however, God changed her name to Sarah, meaning "a queen." It is a marvelous picture of the transition from Old Testament Judaism to New Testament Christianity!

It was the "Sarai" of the Jewish nation who brought forth the Son of God, only then to have her name changed to the "Sarah" of New Testament Christianity — who shall one day fulfill the royal position of her prophetic profile. We shall rule and reign with Christ for 1,000 years as "Sarah," the queen!

Over and over again God has allowed a pattern to emerge from the stories of those whose lives are recorded in the Old Testament in order to show the great master plan of the ages.

Who Is Keturah?

Now the big question: Since Hagar, the bondwoman, is a prophetic profile of Old Testament Judaism, and Sarah, the free woman, is a type of New Testament Christianity, what shall we do with Keturah, the other wife of Abraham? The account is given in Genesis chapter 25:

*"Then again Abraham took a wife, and her name was **Keturah**.*

"And she bare him Zimran, and Jokshan, and Medan, and Midian, and Ishbak, and Shuah" (Genesis 25:1-2).

In verses 5 and 6, we are told that ...

"Abraham gave all that he had unto Isaac.

"But unto the sons of the concubines, which Abraham had, Abraham gave gifts, and sent them away from Isaac his son" (Genesis 25:5-6).

What of Keturah? Could she represent that third great religion which had its roots in Abraham? *Time Magazine* once portrayed the three religions quite vividly on its front cover. The Star of David was drawn to represent the religion of Judaism; the cross was drawn to represent Christianity; and the crest of the moon with a star was drawn to represent Islam. Could these three religions be portrayed prophetically in the lives of Abraham's three wives?

If so, then we should take note that only the son of Sarah was considered to be the heir to Abraham's inheritance. Hagar and her son were cast out with only a little bread and a bottle of water. They received no portion whatsoever in the inheritance. The children of Keturah were also denied an inheritance. Abraham supplied them with gifts, but that's all. He still sent them away. Isaac alone was considered to be the son of promise — and that brings us to his profile.

The Birth of Isaac

Isaac was a type of Christ. There are events in his life that seem to tell a prophetic story. First of all, his birth was a miracle. Sarah, his mother, had long since passed the years of childbearing.

At one point, she became so overly anxious that she talked her husband into producing a son through her bondmaid, Hagar — which, as we have already said, represents the dispensation of *Law*. She was long overdue for a son when Isaac finally came along, and in like manner Jesus Christ was born 4,000 years after Adam.

God had to perform a miracle in the womb of Sarah in order for her to bear a son. God also performed a miracle in the womb of the virgin Mary in order for her to bring forth the Son of God. The miracle birth of Isaac was a type of the miracle birth of Christ.

Just in passing, let me say that Isaac was born when Abraham was 100 years old. Christ on the other hand was born after 4,000 years. The years of Abraham being 100 divides into 4,000 years, leaving the number 40. Now, we believe the number 40 in the Bible represents the number of testing or trial. It is interesting to note that Jesus Christ was born at the end of 100 forty-year periods of testing for the human race. Yes, the birth of Isaac draws a prophetic parallel to the birth of Jesus Christ.

The Offering of Isaac

Then second, there is the story of the offering of Isaac, given in Genesis 22:

"Take now thy son, thine only son Isaac, whom thou lovest, and get thee into the land of Moriah; and offer him there for a burnt-offering upon one of the mountains which I will tell thee of" (Genesis 22:2).

Here is one of the clearest pictures of the crucifixion of Christ to be found in the pages of the Old Testament. Isaac was to be sacrificed by his father. In like manner, *"God so loved the world that he gave his only begotten Son."* It was God who gave His Son for a sacrifice on Calvary.

According to the story, Abraham and his son rose up early in the morning in order to begin their three-day journey to the place of sacrifice.

As they approached Mount Moriah, Abraham ordered his servants to stay and wait. He then took the wood for the burnt offering and laid it upon Isaac.

Please note, just as Isaac bore the wood for the offering to the place of sacrifice, even so our Lord Jesus

Christ bore his cross to the place of crucifixion.

As they approached the place where the sacrifice was to be made, Isaac questioned his father:

"Behold the fire and the wood: but where is the lamb for a burnt-offering?" (Genesis 22:7).

The answer his father gave is one of the most profound prophecies ever uttered:

"And Abraham said, My son, God will provide himself a lamb for a burnt-offering" (Genesis 22:8).

What a statement! It is true that God not only provided a sacrifice for the atonement of sin, but He provided Himself as that sacrifice. Paul wrote:

"To wit, that God was in Christ, reconciling the world unto himself" (II Corinthians 5:19).

In Jesus dwells the fullness of the Godhead bodily. He was more than just a human being born of a virgin, He was God incarnate — God clothed in human flesh. How true the statement, *"God will provide Himself a lamb for a burnt offering."*

The place of sacrifice was called Mount Moriah. It was the high place just above the city of Salem, where Melchizedek ruled not only as king, but also as priest of the Most High God. Evidently, this spot on Mount Moriah had been used for some time as a place of sacrifice in the worship of God.

According to Flavius Josephus, a first-century Jewish historian, Mount Moriah was the same mountain which King David bought for a place of sacrifice, and upon which his son, Solomon, built the First

Temple. Two-thousand years later, that same mountain became the scene of another sacrifice. The place we call Calvary was actually the northern ridge of Mount Moriah.

Most sons would refuse to offer themselves as a sacrifice, but not Isaac. He was willing to lay down his life at the request of his father. This is a prophetic type of Jesus Christ, who willingly came and presented Himself as a sacrifice for the atonement of sin.

In Hebrews 12, we are told of *"Jesus the author and finisher of our faith; who for the joy that was set before him endured the cross ..."* (Hebrews 12:2).

In the Epistle to the Philippians, chapter 2, the Apostle Paul wrote:

"And being found in fashion as a man, he humbled himself, and became obedient unto death, even the death of the cross" (Philippians 2:8).

As Isaac crawled upon the altar that day, he knew only that God had commanded his death. As far as he knew, his life was over. His father, Abraham, had been told to sacrifice his son. God was testing the faith of Abraham. The book of Hebrews informs us:

"By faith Abraham, when he was tried, offered up Isaac: and he that had received the promises offered up his only begotten son,
"Of whom it was said, That in Isaac shall thy seed be called:
"Accounting that God was able to raise him up, even from the dead; from whence also he received him in a figure" (Hebrews 11:17-19).

There are two things in these verses that are quite significant. First of all, the writer of this New Testament book called Isaac the *"only begotten son"* of Abraham. Yet, Abraham had other sons. Isaac was referred to as the *"only begotten son"* of Abraham because he was the only son of promise. In like manner, our Lord Jesus Christ was called *"the only begotten Son"* (John 3:16) of God.

In Exodus 4:22, God called the nation of Israel, His *"firstborn son."* There is no contradiction, however, for Jesus was the Son of Promise. Isaac, then, was a prophetic picture of Jesus Christ, the *"only begotten"* Son of God. Secondly, the writer of our New Testament book of Hebrews, said that Abraham believed in the resurrection:

"Accounting that God was able to raise him up, even from the dead; from whence also he received him in a figure" (Hebrews 11:19).

We are told that Abraham fully expected his son to die, but that he also fully expected his son to be raised from the dead. God had promised that the Messiah would come through Isaac. When Isaac's life was spared at the last moment, it was a prophetic figure of the resurrection — so said the writer of Hebrews.

As Abraham raised his hand that day to take the life of his son, the angel of the Lord stopped him, commended him for his great faith, and then showed him a substitute. Abraham looked up and saw a ram caught in a thicket. In like manner, you and I are the ones who deserved to die on the cross that day when

the Savior became our substitute. He took our place
in death. That is the whole concept of sacrificial
worship. The fact that a lamb was substituted for the
life of Isaac, offers us a prophetic view of the great
substitute who died in our place that we might live
forever.

A Bride for Isaac

Our next prophetic view can be found in the taking
of a bride for Isaac. It is a picture of New Testament
Christianity. We are the "bride" of Christ.

Abraham sent his eldest servant into a far country
in order to fetch a bride for Isaac. The servant is a
type of the Holy Spirit who was sent from heaven to
earth in order to fetch a bride for Jesus. In the Bible,
Abraham's servant remains unnamed. He spoke not
of himself, but of his master and his master's son.
Such is typical of the Holy Spirit. He came to speak
not of Himself, but of the Savior:

*"Howbeit when he, the Spirit of truth, is come, he will guide
you into all truth: for he shall not speak of himself; but whatsoever he shall hear, that shall he speak: and he will show
you things to come.*

*"He shall glorify me: for he shall receive of mine, and shall
show it unto you"* (John 16:13-14).

Though the eldest servant of Abraham remained
unnamed in the Bible, he is given a name in the ancient apocryphal book of *Jasher*. There, he is called
Eliezer. He was sent to the land of Mesopotamia,
unto the city of Nahor, Abraham's brother, to find a
bride for Isaac.

He was instructed not to take a wife from among the daughters of the Canaanites, but to find someone special for Abraham's son. It is important to note that each time a Gentile bride was taken by God's great men, she was no ordinary person.

When Joseph took a Gentile bride, she was the daughter of the High Priest in the land of Egypt. The Gentile bride for Boaz was Ruth, the daughter of the king of Moab. And when the eldest servant of Abraham went to fetch a bride for Isaac, he was not allowed to get just anyone; he was told to look for somebody special. This is a prophetic picture of New Testament Christianity. As the bride of Christ, we are somebody special. We are not to live our lives after the fashion of this world. We should live holy lives, dedicated to the service of the King, for we have been chosen for royalty.

When Eliezer came near the city of Nahor, he stopped by a well and asked the Lord to help him choose the right girl. He prayed:

"And let it come to pass, that the damsel to whom I shall say, Let down thy pitcher, I pray thee, that I may drink; and she shall say, Drink, and I will give thy camels drink also: let the same be she that thou hast appointed for thy servant Isaac; and thereby shall I know that thou hast showed kindness unto my master" (Genesis 24:14).

Before he was even able to finish the prayer, a young lady by the name of Rebekah approached. She went down to the well and filled her pitcher. When Eliezer asked her for a drink of water, she not only complied, but also offered to draw water for his camels. Of course, the servant was thrilled that his prayer had been so soon answered.

Please note that the characteristic which set Rebekah apart from the others was the fact that she was kind, generous, and industrious. Those are the kind of characteristics God is looking for today. God did not pick a lazy person for the son of Abraham. Neither is God the Holy Spirit going to choose that kind of person for Jesus.

Happy with his find, he gave Rebekah a golden earring and two bracelets. Then he went to her home, met Abraham's brother, Laban, and asked for her hand in marriage. The final decision, however, lay with Rebekah. When she was asked, *"Wilt thou go with this man?"* she answered, *"I will go."* In like manner, the Holy Spirit invites you to receive Christ as Savior, but the final decision is yours.

What happened next is a prophetic view of the Rapture. The servant took Rebekah to the Promised Land. Isaac came from the south country in hopes of seeing the caravan. It was evening time when they met. Rebekah veiled her face, dismounted her camel, and went out into the field to meet the man, whom having not seen, she loved. Isaac took her home to become his wife. It is a beautiful picture of that day when you and I hear the shout and the trumpet sound. The Holy Spirit will take us home to meet the one whom having not seen, we love.

The name Rebekah means "to fetter or capture." She was so beautiful as to capture the heart of her bridegroom. Prophetically, she is a type of New Testament Christianity. We are special people loved by the Lord.

Jacob and Esau

Finally, Rebekah bore twin sons — Jacob and Esau. Since Rebekah is a type of New Testament Christianity, Jacob and Esau must be typical of the offspring. Over the past 2,000 years of Church history, one can see those two basic characteristics. Just as the firstborn, Esau, was a general disappointment to his parents, even so, one of the forms of organized Christianity has become a general disappointment to the ministry of Christ around the world.

Just as the younger Jacob, became the greater, even so, evangelical Christianity has been blessed of God, and has done a great work in spreading the Gospel throughout the world. Perhaps soon the spiritual counterpart of Rebekah will be taken home to the Father's house to meet the darling of Heaven — the one, whom having not seen, we love.

Chapter Four

The Rejected Joseph

The story of Joseph is one of the clearest portrayals of Christ to be found in the pages of the Old Testament. There are many comparisons between the life of Joseph and his prophetic counterpart. Some of those similarities will be pointed out in this study.

The story begins in the 30th chapter of Genesis. Could that be a cryptic juxtaposition of Scripture — a reminder that Christ would begin His ministry at age 30? Typical of Christ, Joseph also began his ministry as the governor of Egypt at the age of 30.

In previous studies on the 22 letters of the Hebrew alphabet, we noticed that each successive chapter in Genesis follows the meaning ascribed to a corresponding Hebrew letter. Chapter 1 follows the theme of the first letter, *aleph* [א], chapter 2 corresponds with *beit* [ב], chapter 3 with *gimel* [ג], etc. Chapter

23 repeats the alphabetic design starting with a subject that corresponds with the meaning of *aleph* [א], chapter 24 with *beit* [ב], etc. Therefore, chapter 30 appears to be a *chet* [ח] chapter. The Hebrew letter, *chet* [ח] refers to a "new beginning" and "transcendence." The story of Joseph begins in the chapter which corresponds to the letter of "new beginning." It is a remarkable reminder of the greater picture — the First Advent of Christ. Our Savior introduced a new beginning for all who will believe in Him. His death and resurrection offers a transcendence "from death unto life" for us:

"Verily, verily, I say unto you, He that heareth my word, and believeth on him that sent me, hath everlasting life, and shall not come into condemnation; but is passed from death unto life" (John 5:24).

Twenty Chapters Tell the Story

Chapters 30-50 present a prophetic foreview of Christ and His ministry. Could these 20 chapters be another divine juxtaposition of Scripture — indicative of 20 centuries? So far, it has taken this long to tell the story of Christ. From the First Coming of Christ to the promise of His kingdom, almost 2,000 years have come and gone. We do not know if those years have any prophetic connection with the story of Joseph, but they are close enough to at least warrant a comparison.

His Miracle Birth

The birth of Joseph, like the Savior's birth, took a miracle to make it happen:

"And God remembered Rachel, and God hearkened to her, and opened her womb.

"And she conceived, and bare a son; and said, God hath taken away my reproach:

"And she called his name Joseph; and said, The LORD shall add to me another son" (Genesis 30:22-24).

This was no ordinary birth. Rachel was barren. God had to perform a miracle in her womb in order for Joseph to be conceived and delivered. When she finally gave birth to Joseph, she said, *"God hath taken away my reproach"* (v.23). In a similar manner, Christ was not the product of an earthly father. He was born of a virgin. His father was God Himself! God performed a miracle in the womb of Mary in order for her to bare the *"only begotten"* Son of God.

Right at the beginning of Joseph's story, we are introduced to his prophetic nature. We are told about his miracle birth. At Joseph's birth, no one realized that he would grow up to become their savior. In like manner, at Christ's First Advent, Israel did not recognize that He would take away their reproach as well. Like the story of Joseph, that will become clear at His Second Advent.

Jacob's Favorite Wife

Joseph was the son of Rachel, Jacob's favorite wife. In like manner, Christ was the product of Israel, God's favorite wife. The very name of God's wife was taken from Jacob, whose name was changed to Israel.

According to Justin Martyr (b. A.D. 110), the second-century Gentile Christian theologian, Leah represents Judaism while Rachel represents New Testament Christianity.

Rachel's name, meaning "ewe lamb," lends to the view that Joseph was born as a lamb. In like manner, Christ was the "lamb of God." This symbol is also used of God's people. We are like sheep. Christ is the Great Shepherd. Rachel also bore Benjamin whose name means "son of my right hand." In later years, Solomon's Temple was located in his territory.

Leah's name, meaning "a wild cow," also has prophetic overtones. Her sons were Reuben, Simeon, Levi, Judah, Issachar, and Zebulun. Judah was the one through whom the Messiah would be born, and Levi would beget the priesthood. Under the Mosaic Law, a red heifer was sacrificed for the spiritual cleansing of the people. Perhaps Leah was somehow represented by the heifer. After all, she was named for a heifer and her sister, Rachel, was named for a lamb. These two sacrificial animals prophetically represent both Israel and Christ.

Josephus tells a strange story that occurred shortly before the destruction of Herod's Temple. The high priest was about to lead a heifer out of the Temple courtyard to the place of sacrifice on Mt. Olivet. It had been properly examined and found to qualify for the sacrifice. According to the Mosaic Law, the red heifer had to be a virgin. Furthermore, it had to be genetically pure having no white or black hairs. As the high priest approached the animal, it gave birth to a lamb! Josephus said the story was absolutely true. The virgin heifer gave birth to a lamb! What a miracle! God was evidently telling them that Israel (the heifer) had given birth to the Messiah (the lamb).

Bilhah, Rachel's handmaiden, bore Dan and Naphtali. Her name means "foolish." Her firstborn, Dan, was to become a *"... serpent by the way, an adder in the path, that biteth the horse heels, so that his rider shall fall backward"* (Genesis 49:17). Many scholars believe this is a reference to the Antichrist. He was born from a mother named "Foolish!"

Zilpah, Leah's handmaiden, bore Gad and Asher. Her name means "a drop." Gad refers to "a troop" and Asher means "blessing."

Abraham, Isaac, Jacob, and Joseph

Some scholars suggest that Abraham, Isaac, Jacob, and Joseph are typical of "four successive steps in God's program of redemption." Abraham is a type of sovereign election by grace; Isaac represents selective calling; Jacob exemplifies salvation by grace alone; and Joseph is a picture of glorification. God revealed this plan through Paul, who may have had them in mind as he wrote:

"... whom he did predestinate, them he also called: and whom he called, them he also justified: and whom he justified, them he also glorified" (Romans 8:30).

A reflection upon the lives of these men bears out the truth of God's plan. Abram was chosen from a wicked society of idolaters following the Tower of Babel debacle. There were no redeeming features to Abram's life that merited God's favor. He was predestinated — chosen by grace.

Isaac was selected instead of Ishmael. He was the son of promise, born of a free woman while Ishmael was born of a slave. Abraham also had sons by Keturah, but only Isaac received the inheritance. In spite of Isaac's efforts to pass his inheritance on to Esau, Jacob was God's clear choice. Though the narrative shows no redeeming features, God loved Jacob and hated Esau. He chose Jacob by grace alone.

Finally, Joseph exhibits glorification. The favorite son of Jacob was despised and rejected by his brothers. Yet, in the end, he was exalted as the ruler who sat at the right hand of Pharaoh and, at that time, presided over a world empire. What a prophetic progression! What a blessed hope for all believers! We, too, await glorification!

The Meaning of His Name

Joseph's name [יוסף] means, "He [God] will add."
This, too, is representative of the ministry of Christ.
From His death, burial and resurrection have come
millions upon millions of believers — the *"born
again."* Christ was the *"firstfruits"* of all those who
believe:

*"But now is Christ risen from the dead, and become the
firstfruits of them that slept"* (I Corinthians 15:20).

Through Him, we have been added to the family of
God. As Adam was the great subtractor, the last Adam
is the great multiplier:

*"Except a corn of wheat fall into the ground and die, it
abideth alone: but if it die, it bringeth forth much fruit"*
(John 12:24).

The name Joseph was given to him by his earthly
parents. Likewise, Jesus received His name from
Mary. Under these names, both were rejected by their
own people. However, Joseph was finally exalted to
the right hand of Pharaoh and given a new name —
one of exaltation:

*"And Pharaoh took off his ring from his hand, and put it
upon Joseph's hand ...*
*"And he made him to ride in the second chariot which he
had; and they cried before him, Bow the knee: and he made
him ruler over all the land of Egypt.*
"And Pharaoh called Joseph's name **Zaphnath-
paaneah...**" (Genesis 41:42,43,45).

Joseph had two names. Joseph, meaning "adding
to" or "increasing," points to God's earthly plan to

increase the number of believers worldwide. Zaphnath-paaneah, meaning "revealer of secrets," points directly to the book of Revelation. We are told:

"Eye hath not seen, nor ear heard, neither have entered into the heart of man, the things which God hath prepared for them that love him" (I Cor. 2:9).

We see through a *"glass, darkly"* (I Cor. 13:12) — awaiting the day of His revealing.

After Christ suffered death on the cross, He rose again and ascended into heaven, where He sat down at the right hand of the Father. When He comes again, we will learn that Christ has a new name:

"His eyes were as a flame of fire, and on his head were many crowns; and he had a name written, that no man knew, but he himself" (Revelation 19:12).

Christ is the greater "revealer of secrets."

He Witnessed Their Wickedness

Joseph saw the wickedness of his brothers and reported it to his father.

"These are the generations of Jacob. Joseph, being seventeen years old, was feeding the flock with his brethren; and the lad was with the sons of Bilhah, and with the sons of Zilpah, his father's wives: and Joseph brought unto his father their evil report" (Genesis 37:2).

In like manner, Jesus testified against the wickedness of the world:

"The world cannot hate you; but me it hateth, because I testify of it, that the works thereof are evil" (John 7:7).

The Beloved Son

Joseph was the beloved of his father:

"Now Israel loved Joseph more than all his children, because he was the son of his old age: and he made him a coat of many colors" (Genesis 37:3).

Jesus was also the well-beloved son of the *"Ancient of Days."* God announced this at the baptism of Christ:

"And lo a voice from heaven, saying, This is my beloved Son, in whom I am well pleased" (Matthew 3:17).

Again, on the Mount of Transfiguration, God spoke to Peter, James, and John:

"While he yet spake, behold, a bright cloud overshadowed them: and behold a voice out of the cloud, which said, This is my beloved Son, in whom I am well pleased; hear ye him" (Matthew 17:5).

The Dreams

Joseph was a dreamer — a foreteller of his future. First, Joseph saw his brothers as sheaves of grain bowing down to him. In another dream, he saw the sun, moon, and eleven stars making obeisance to him.

In the first dream, the field of grain focuses on Israel and speaks of Christ's earthly kingdom. In the second dream, the starry heavens focus on the Church and speak of Christ's heavenly kingdom.

Rejection

Joseph, the beloved of the father, was sent to visit his brothers. Jacob was interested in their welfare:

"And he said to him, Go, I pray thee, see whether it be well with thy brethren, and well with the flocks; and bring me word again. So he sent him out of the vale of Hebron, and he came to Shechem" (Genesis 37:14).

The brothers had been at Shechem, meaning "fellowship," but they moved to Dothan, meaning "law." Joseph found them in the land of law. When they saw him, they were filled with hatred:

"... Behold, this dreamer cometh."
"Come now therefore, and let us slay him, and cast him into some pit, and we will say, Some evil beast hath devoured him: and we shall see what will become of his dreams" (Genesis 37:19,20).

In like manner, Christ was rejected:

"He was in the world, and the world was made by him, and the world knew him not.
"He came unto his own, and his own received him not.
"But as many as received him, to them gave he power to become the sons of God, even to them that believe on his name:
"Which were born, not of blood, nor of the will of the flesh, nor of the will of man, but of God" (John 1:10-13).

Isaiah predicted His rejection as well:

"He is despised and rejected of men; a man of sorrows, and acquainted with grief: and we hid as it were our faces from him; he was despised, and we esteemed him not.
"Surely he hath borne our griefs, and carried our sorrows: yet we did esteem him stricken, smitten of God, and afflicted.
"But he was wounded for our transgressions, he was bruised

for our iniquities: the chastisement of our peace was upon him; and with his stripes we are healed" (Isaiah 53:3-5).

Sold for Silver

Joseph's brothers, led by Judah, sold him for 20 pieces of silver:

"And Judah said unto his brethren, What profit is it if we slay our brother, and conceal his blood?

"Come, and let us sell him to the Ishmeelites, and let not our hand be upon him; for he is our brother and our flesh. And his brethren were content.

"Then there passed by Midianites merchantmen; and they drew and lifted up Joseph out of the pit, and sold Joseph to the Ishmeelites for twenty pieces of silver: and they brought Joseph into Egypt" (Genesis 37:26-28).

It is remarkable that a man named Judas repeated the disgusting deed some 1,800 years later. He betrayed Jesus for 30 pieces of silver:

"And said unto them, What will ye give me, and I will deliver him unto you? And they covenanted with him for thirty pieces of silver" (Matthew 26:15).

Cast Into a Pit

When Joseph arrived, his brothers treated him roughly. They stripped him of his coat of many colors and threw him into a pit:

"And it came to pass, when Joseph was come unto his brethren, that they stript Joseph out of his coat, his coat of many colors that was on him;

"And they took him, and cast him into a pit: and the pit was empty, there was no water in it" (Genesis 37:23,24).

Joseph's brothers later dipped the coat of many colors in blood, and presented it to their father. In like manner, Christ was stripped of his clothes:

"Then the soldiers, when they had crucified Jesus, took his garments, and made four parts, to every soldier a part; and also his coat: now the coat was without seam, woven from the top throughout.

"They said therefore among themselves, Let us not rend it, but cast lots for it, whose it shall be: that the scripture might be fulfilled, which saith, They parted my raiment among them, and for my vesture they did cast lots. These things therefore the soldiers did" (John 19:23-24).

When Christ returns, He will be wearing His vesture dipped in blood:

"And he was clothed with a vesture dipped in blood" (Revelation 19:13).

Joseph was cast into the pit to die, but he came out from the place of death alive. In like manner, Christ was placed in a tomb — a place of death — but was resurrected.

Taken to Egypt

Joseph escaped death by being sold into slavery and taken to Egypt. Christ was also taken into Egypt to escape death. Speaking of both Israel and Christ, Hosea wrote:

"When Israel was a child, then I loved him, and called my son out of Egypt" (Hosea 11:1).

Matthew shows how this verse also refers to Christ:

"And was there until the death of Herod: that it might be fulfilled which was spoken of the Lord by the prophet, saying,

Out of Egypt have I called my son" (Matthew 2:15).

Egypt is typical of the world. As Joseph ruled over Egypt, someday Christ will rule over all nations.

He Became a Servant

In Egypt, Joseph was sold to Potiphar as a servant.

"And Joseph was brought down to Egypt; and Potiphar, an officer of Pharaoh, captain of the guard, an Egyptian, bought him of the hands of the Ishmeelites, which had brought him down thither.

"And the LORD was with Joseph, and he was a prosperous man; and he was in the house of his master the Egyptian.

"And his master saw that the LORD was with him, and that the LORD made all that he did to prosper in his hand.

"And Joseph found grace in his sight, and he served him: and he made him overseer over his house, and all that he had he put into his hand" (Genesis 39:1-4).

In like manner, Christ took upon Himself the form of a servant:

"Who, being in the form of God, thought it not robbery to be equal with God:

"But made himself of no reputation, and took upon him the form of a servant, and was made in the likeness of men:

"And being found in fashion as a man, he humbled himself, and became obedient unto death, even the death of the cross.

"Wherefore God also hath highly exalted him, and given him a name which is above every name:

"That at the name of Jesus every knee should bow" (Philippians 2:6-10).

Like Joseph, those years as a servant did not last. Christ will be exalted to rulership. However, Christ's kingdom will be much greater and last forever.

Numbered With Transgressors

Joseph was falsely accused by Potiphar's wife and cast into prison. There, he was numbered with transgressors. In like manner, Christ was falsely accused. At Calvary, Christ was suspended between two thieves. Isaiah predicted:

"Therefore will I divide him a portion with the great, and he shall divide the spoil with the strong; because he hath poured out his soul unto death: and he was numbered with the transgressors; and he bare the sin of many, and made intercession for the transgressors" (Isaiah 53:12).

Mark described the scene at Calvary and reported the fulfillment of Isaiah's prophecy:

"And the scripture was fulfilled, which saith, And he was numbered with the transgressors" (Mark 15:28).

Savior and Judge

Joseph was declared guilty on the word of a scorned woman. He was sent to languish in an Egyptian prison. It was not long until his leadership characteristics caught the attention of the keeper. Soon, Joseph became his deputy. In time, Pharaoh cast his butler and baker into the prison. Joseph became the savior of the butler and judge of the baker. In like manner, Jesus is the Savior for all who will believe the Gospel, but will become the Judge for all who refuse.

Seven Years of Famine

The baker was executed, but the butler was returned to his position in Pharaoh's court. Two years went by and the butler forgot about Joseph. One day Pharaoh became distraught over a series of dreams. He sought the counsel of his wise men, but they could not interpret them. At that point, the butler remembered his promise to Joseph. He told Pharaoh about Joseph's ability to interpret dreams. Joseph was promptly called:

"And Pharaoh said unto Joseph, In my dream, behold, I stood upon the bank of the river:

"And, behold, there came up out of the river seven kine, fatfleshed and well favored; and they fed in a meadow:

"And, behold, seven other kine came up after them, poor and very ill favored and leanfleshed, such as I never saw in all the land of Egypt for badness:

"And the lean and the ill favored kine did eat up the first seven fat kine:

"And when they had eaten them up, it could not be known that they had eaten them; but they were still ill favored, as at the beginning. So I awoke.

"And I saw in my dream, and, behold, seven ears came up in one stalk, full and good:

"And, behold, seven ears, withered, thin, and blasted with the east wind, sprung up after them:

"And the thin ears devoured the seven good ears: and I told this unto the magicians; but there was none that could declare it to me.

"And Joseph said unto Pharaoh, The dream of Pharaoh is one: God hath showed Pharaoh what he is about to do.

"The seven good kine are seven years; and the seven good ears are seven years: the dream is one.

"And the seven thin and ill favored kine that came up after them are seven years; and the seven empty ears blasted with the east wind shall be seven years of famine.

"This is the thing which I have spoken unto Pharaoh: What God is about to do he showeth unto Pharaoh.

"Behold, there come seven years of great plenty throughout all the land of Egypt:

"And there shall arise after them seven years of famine; and all the plenty shall be forgotten in the land of Egypt; and the famine shall consume the land" (Genesis 41:17-30).

Joseph's remarkable interpretation landed him the position as governor over all the land of Egypt. It became Joseph's job to oversee the storage of grain in preparation for the coming famine. This is a major part of the story. Prophetically, Egypt's famine represents a future worldwide famine — seven years of tribulation — during which Christ will judge the world. The Tribulation Period is a prominent feature of prophecy. Daniel presents it as the concluding seven-year "week" of seventy sabbatical cycles:

"And he shall confirm the covenant with many for one week: and in the midst of the week he shall cause the sacrifice and the oblation to cease, and for the overspreading of abominations he shall make it desolate, even until the consummation, and that determined shall be poured upon the desolate" (Daniel 9:27).

A sabbatical cycle runs for seven years. Gabriel showed Daniel that Israel's future would be characterized by these cycles. They are an integral part of God's plan for Israel. During that time, God's Chosen People will come face to face with the sin of rejecting their Messiah. They will be drawn inexorably to Christ — just as the story of Joseph portrays.

A Gentile Bride

Pharaoh handpicked Joseph's Gentile bride. Her name was Asenath, a title that means, "she who is of Neith." In other words, this woman had been dedicated by her priestly father to Neith, the Egyptian goddess of wisdom, art, and craft. This goddess corresponds with the Greek goddess Athena and the Roman, Minerva. She was also connected with the idea of defensive protection, and in Graeco-Roman art was usually shown clad in a helmet.

As a type of Christ, Joseph took a Gentile bride, foreshadowing the later work of the Lord during the age of the Church. Historical tradition says that she became a follower of her husband's God.

Her father, Poti-pherah, was a priest in the sacred city of On, known in the Greek language as Heliopolis, or "city of the sun." From the earliest days of Egypt, this temple-city was dedicated to the worship of the sun god. Its priests were said to be the most learned in all Egypt. They were masters of astronomy, mathematics, and philosophy. Their chief priest held the title, "Greatest of Seers." Joseph's father-in-law was probably the holder of this title.

The Unrecognized Brother

Back in Canaan, Joseph's family was unprepared for the famine. The brothers were forced to look to Gentiles for help. Soon, they journeyed down to Egypt in search of supplies. As they stood before the governor, little did they know that he was their rejected brother. They did not recognize him, but Joseph knew them. Lest they recognize his voice, he spoke to them through an interpreter. Here, the story really gets interesting. Before he would identify himself they must be put in a position of confessing their crime:

"And Joseph was the governor over the land, and he it was that sold to all the people of the land: and Joseph's brethren came, and bowed down themselves before him with their faces to the earth.

"And Joseph saw his brethren, and he knew them, but made himself strange unto them, and spake roughly unto them; and he said unto them, Whence come ye? And they said, From the land of Canaan to buy food.

"And Joseph knew his brethren, but they knew not him.

"And Joseph remembered the dreams which he dreamed of them, and said unto them, Ye are spies; to see the nakedness of the land ye are come" (Genesis 42:6-9).

Joseph quizzed them about their family, including questions about his younger brother, Benjamin. Then he threw them in jail for three days:

"And he put them all together into ward three days.

"And Joseph said unto them the third day, This do, and live; for I fear God:

"If ye be true men, let one of your brethren be bound in the house of your prison: go ye, carry corn for the famine of your houses:

"But bring your youngest brother unto me; so shall your words be verified, and ye shall not die. And they did so.

"And they said one to another, We are verily guilty concerning our brother, in that we saw the anguish of his soul, when he besought us, and we would not hear; therefore is this distress come upon us.

"And Reuben answered them, saying, Spake I not unto you, saying, Do not sin against the child; and ye would not hear? therefore, behold, also his blood is required.

"And they knew not that Joseph understood them; for he spake unto them by an interpreter.

"And he turned himself about from them, and wept; and returned to them again, and communed with them, and took from them Simeon, and bound him before their eyes" (Genesis 42:17-24).

Three days of incarceration are indicative of Israel's captivities and dispersion over the past three millennia. Moses, who recounted this story of Joseph, also introduced the concept that a day could represent a thousand years:

"For a thousand years in thy sight are but as yesterday when it is past, and as a watch in the night" (Psalm 90:4).

This concept is consistent throughout Moses' writings. Often when days are mentioned, they appear to have prophetic implications to millennia. This much we know — Israel has suffered over the past three-thousand years.

On the third day, Joseph revealed his terms. They would return to Canaan with food for their families, but on their next trip to Egypt, they must bring their younger brother, Benjamin. To insure their return, the governor would keep a hostage — Simeon!

Simeon means "hearing." This is a prophetic scenario suggesting that the Chosen People would return to the Promised Land without their spiritual hearing. There are many Scriptures which teach that Israel will not understand God's grand plan. To this day, Jewish ears are deaf to the Messiahship of Jesus. Simeon's incarceration set the prophetic precedent for Jewish misunderstanding of New Testament concepts. In my book, *Hidden Prophecies in the Song of Moses*, I dealt with Simeon's prophetic meaning. It sets the theme for the Song of Moses which begins in Deuteronomy 32 and concludes in Psalms 90-100. Together they comprise twelve stanzas — each designating a tribe. But Psalms 90-100 were removed, leaving Deuteronomy 32, which represents Simeon, somewhat "incarcerated" under the Mosaic Law.

Spiritual deafness came to Israel. In Isaiah 6, the prophet was commissioned to:

"... Go, and tell this people, Hear ye indeed, but understand not; and see ye indeed, but perceive not.

"Make the heart of this people fat, and make their ears heavy, and shut their eyes; lest they see with their eyes, and hear with their ears, and understand with their heart, and convert, and be healed" (Isaiah 6:9-10).

Jesus taught in parables to veil the true meaning of His teachings. Concluding His stories, Jesus said:

"Who hath ears to hear, let him hear.

"And the disciples came, and said unto him, Why speakest thou unto them in parables?

"He answered and said unto them, Because it is given unto you to know the mysteries of the kingdom of heaven, but to them it is not given" (Matthew 13:9-11).

At the conclusion of each of the seven letters to the Churches in Revelation 2 and 3, John writes:

"He that hath an ear, let him hear what the Spirit saith unto the churches" (Revelation 2:7).

The spiritual deafness of Israel continues to this day. During the Tribulation Period, they will be brought face to face with their unbelief and realize that Jesus Christ was and is their Messiah.

Benjamin

The brothers were sent home to fetch Benjamin. Joseph was particularly concerned for Benjamin because he was his only full-blood brother, born of his mother, Rachel. Joseph wanted to know if the brothers had treated Benjamin like they had treated him. Benjamin is also a prophetic type of Christ.

At his birth, Rachel named him *Benoni*, meaning "son of my sorrow." Later, Jacob changed his name to *Benjamin*, meaning "son of my right hand." Both names are indicative of Christ. He was "a man of sorrows, and acquainted with grief" (Isaiah 53:3). However, when He returned to heaven, He sat down at the right hand of the Father on high.

Rachel

Rachel's name, meaning "ewe," denotes a sacrifice. Perhaps that is why she died in childbirth. Her sad end became a prophecy pointing to the prophetic "birthpangs of travail." It was a term used by the prophets concerning the end-time. Jesus explained this to His disciples:

"A woman when she is in travail hath sorrow, because her hour is come: but as soon as she is delivered of the child, she remembereth no more the anguish, for joy that a man is born into the world.

"And ye now therefore have sorrow: but I will see you again, and your heart shall rejoice, and your joy no man taketh from you" (John 16:21,22).

Jesus also referred to the prophetic signs of wars, disease, famine, and earthquakes as birthpangs of the end of the age:

"For nation shall rise against nation, and kingdom against kingdom: and there shall be famines, and pestilences, and earthquakes, in divers places.
"All these are the beginning of sorrows" (Matthew 24:7,8).

The Banquet

Upon their return to Egypt, Joseph invited them to a meal at his home. Simeon was returned. They are now prepared to understand what is happening. In due time, they will be told. Joseph is anxious to assure them of their salvation. Each brother was seated in the order of his birth and the men marveled at one another. Food was served, but Benjamin received five times more than the others.

The Cup

The following day, the brothers were prepared to leave for home. Little did they know that Joseph was not yet through with them. He had a steward hide his cup in Benjamin's sack. Outside of town, Egyptian soldiers stopped them, searched, and found the sacred vessel. This brought extreme grief to the brothers. They feared for their lives. The tale of the cup seems to have prophetic significance. On the night before His crucifixion, Jesus took a cup of wine and likened it to His blood. He then passed it among His disciples encouraging them to partake. Later, in the Garden of Gethsemane, He prayed that the cup might pass from Him. The Savior's blood determined destiny — as did the cup found in Benjamin's sack. It was Joseph's cup that brought the brothers back to Joseph. In like manner, it is the cup of Christ's blood that will bring Israel back to their Messiah.

The Confession

Joseph pressed them to confess their guilt concerning him and express love for their father. Judah was the one to confess. He was the leader whose name became indicative of all the tribes — Jew. He spoke for his brothers as he pleaded for grace and mercy:

"And thy servant my father said unto us, Ye know that my wife bare me two sons:
"And the one went out from me, and I said, Surely he is torn in pieces; and I saw him not since:
"And if ye take this also from me, and mischief befall him, ye shall bring down my gray hairs with sorrow to the grave.
"Now therefore when I come to thy servant my father, and the lad be not with us; seeing that his life is bound up in the lad's life;
"It shall come to pass, when he seeth that the lad is not with us, that he will die: and thy servants shall bring down the gray hairs of thy servant our father with sorrow to the grave" (Genesis 44:27-31).

Joseph's purpose was accomplished. They had confessed their sin. He now reveals himself to them:

"Then Joseph could not refrain himself before all them that stood by him; and he cried, Cause every man to go out from me. And there stood no man with him, while Joseph made

himself known unto his brethren.

"And he wept aloud: and the Egyptians and the house of Pharaoh heard.

"And Joseph said unto his brethren, I am Joseph; doth my father yet live? And his brethren could not answer him; for they were troubled at his presence.

"And Joseph said unto his brethren, Come near to me, I pray you. And they came near. And he said, I am Joseph your brother, whom ye sold into Egypt.

"Now therefore be not grieved, nor angry with yourselves, that ye sold me hither: for God did send me before you to preserve life.

"For these two years hath the famine been in the land: and yet there are five years, in the which there shall neither be earing nor harvest.

"And God sent me before you to preserve you a posterity in the earth, and to save your lives by a great deliverance.

"So now it was not you that sent me hither, but God: and he hath made me a father to Pharaoh, and lord of all his house, and a ruler throughout all the land of Egypt.

"Haste ye, and go up to my father, and say unto him, Thus saith thy son Joseph, God hath made me lord of all Egypt: come down unto me, tarry not" (Genesis 45:1-9).

Joseph freely forgives them. These despised Hebrews are to be favored above all the people because their brother is on the throne. This has a dispensational application to the nation of Israel. Joseph and his brothers are an allegory of God's great program for the nation of Israel. During the Tribulation Period, Israel will suffer terribly. Having been forsaken by all nations, Israel will face genocide. During the battle of Armageddon, with nowhere else to turn, they will pray to the one whom their forefathers rejected. Jesus has been waiting a long time to hear that prayer. That's when He will return and save His people.

The Shepherd

Jacob and his sons finally move to Egypt with their entire households and are given the fertile delta of the Nile for grazing their sheep and cattle. Upon arrival, Joseph instructs the brothers to tell Pharaoh that they are shepherds. This, too, has prophetic overtones. There are five shepherds in the Bible who are typical of Christ: Abel was the sacrificing shepherd giving his life and shedding his blood at the hands of his own brother; Jacob was the toiling shepherd who left his father's house to dwell in a far country, fleeing from the wrath of his brother; Joseph was the exalted shepherd who, rejected by his brethren, became the savior of men during the famine; Moses was the delivering shepherd; and David was the royal reigning shepherd.

Egyptian history does not directly mention Joseph, but it does relate the history of the Hyksos — or shepherd kings. They appeared in Egypt about the same time of the Genesis story. Could the original shepherd king be Joseph? We are told that his brothers were given the land of Goshen in the fertile delta of the Nile because they were shepherds:

"And the men are shepherds, for their trade hath been to feed cattle; and they have brought their flocks, and their herds, and all that they have" (Genesis 46:32).

They kept sheep and cattle. These happened to be the very animals represented by Rachel and Leah.

Joseph in the New Testament

The story of Joseph is recounted in Acts 7:9-14. Please note what Stephen said about Joseph being revealed the "second time:"

"And the patriarchs, moved with envy, sold Joseph into Egypt: but God was with him,

"And delivered him out of all his afflictions, and gave him favor and wisdom in the sight of Pharaoh king of Egypt; and he made him governor over Egypt and all his house.

"Now there came a dearth over all the land of Egypt and Canaan, and great affliction: and our fathers found no sustenance.

"But when Jacob heard that there was corn in Egypt, he sent out our fathers first.

"And at the second time Joseph was made known to his brethren; and Joseph's kindred was made known unto Pharaoh.

"Then sent Joseph, and called his father Jacob to him, and all his kindred, threescore and fifteen souls" (Acts 7:9-14).

We are not told in the New Testament that Joseph was an allegory of Christ, but the implication could not be clearer. Just as Joseph was revealed to his brothers the "second time," Christ will be revealed to the Jews at His Second Advent. The story of Joseph not only reveals the First Advent of Christ, but His return to establish the long-looked-for kingdom. God forgave Joseph's brothers, but the plan did not allow an excuse for their wickedness. They suffered, but in the end, were given the fertile land of Goshen. God's forgiveness is a hard truth to accept and difficult for the brothers. After Jacob's death, they were fearful that Joseph would seek revenge. However, their fears were groundless.

"And when Joseph's brethren saw that their father was dead, they said, Joseph will peradventure hate us, and will certainly requite us all the evil which we did unto him.

"And they sent a messenger unto Joseph, saying, Thy father did command before he died, saying,

"So shall ye say unto Joseph, Forgive, I pray thee now, the trespass of thy brethren, and their sin; for they did unto thee evil: and now, we pray thee, forgive the trespass of the servants of the God of thy father. And Joseph wept when they spake unto him.

"And his brethren also went and fell down before his face; and they said, Behold, we be thy servants.

"And Joseph said unto them, Fear not: for am I in the place of God?

"But as for you, ye thought evil against me; but God meant it unto good, to bring to pass, as it is this day, to save much people alive" (Genesis 50:15-20).

It is hard for some people to accept the fact that God freely forgives, but He does. Salvation has no strings attached. We are forgiven because of the blood of Christ, Who died once for all. We need not fear falling from God's grace. Joseph is clear about his forgiveness to the brothers and thus, presents a prophetic message to us about the love of Christ. There is no greater picture of Christ to be found in the pages of the Old Testament.

Chapter Five

The Suffering of Job

The story of Job offers insight into one of the great mysteries of life. The account of his suffering has brought comfort and hope over the centuries to many a person perplexed with the heartaches of life. The book raises the age-old question on whether suffering is a punishment for sin or a development of one's character. Most agree that Job is a classic study on how to endure the dark times of life, but few have ever considered the possibility that the book also presents a prophetic study as well.

Does not all of the Bible weave a singular pattern presenting God's ancient plan of the ages? Like the other prophecies of the Bible, God used the story of Job to demonstrate a prophetic scenario of that which would befall His Chosen People.

The Hebrew term, Job, means "the persecuted one," and like that ancient sufferer, the Jews have endured more agony than any other race or nationality in history. The Jew has certainly been "the persecuted one." The world has always been quick to ridicule the Jew.

The Israelites have always been like a square peg in a round hole — the misfits of humanity — not because of some inferiority, quite the contrary. The Jew has been persecuted in spite of his great contributions to humanity in the fields of art, music, law, government, economics, medicine, science and religion. The world has been abundantly blessed because of Abraham's seed, but they do not recognize it, nor do they accept it. Sad to say, there are whole nations that consider the Jew to be like a cancer that must be eliminated from the human race.

From time to time, I receive letters across my desk from people who suggest that I stop taking the side of those "murderous Jews." In fact, some seem to think that the Jews are responsible for the continuing conflict with the Arabs. Not for a moment do they consider placing the blame on those who pull the triggers.

They blame the Jews for everything! They do not care that it was a Jew who invented the telephone, the television, and many of the miracles of modern medicine. They don't blame the Arabs for bringing the world to the brink of Armageddon, they blame it on the Jews!

There are some who suggest that today's Jews are not even Jews. They promote the theory that the tribes were lost to history. Some have attempted to trace their migration into Europe, believing the ancient Israelites became the progenitors of the British, French, Germans, etc.

Still others believe that the Indians of North America were the descendants of the "ten lost tribes." It seems that everybody is a Jew but the Jew. When it comes to suffering, however, there is no doubt who wins first prize. Let us observe the life of Job and consider the possibility that his life was a prophetic profile of suffering Israel.

So, Was Job a Gentile?

Some rabbis suggest that Job was a Gentile — one of the very few they could accept as a righteous man, having lived long before Moses. But was he really a Gentile? The fact that Job lived another 140 years after his restoration seems to suggest that he lived as a contemporary with others in the Bible, who lived to be between 100 and 150 years old. It is quite possible that he lived during those years when Jacob joined Joseph in Egypt. So why should he have to be a Gentile? Allow me to suggest that he could have been the very person listed in Genesis 46 as one of the sons of Issachar who accompanied Jacob into Egypt:

"And the sons of Issachar; Tola, and Phuvah, and Job ..." (Genesis 46:13).

Jacob's family settled in the land of Goshen, an area covering the fertile delta of the Nile. Job must have been one of those seventy people who accompanied the patriarch into Egypt, otherwise the earliest collection of Hebrew Scriptures would not have included the story of his life. It does not seem reasonable that the story of a Gentile should be included in an otherwise Jewish book.

If Job was appeared before Moses, then the book could have been written in Egypt. The statement in chapter 1, verse 3, wherein Job is called "... *the greatest of all the men of the east,*" may simply be a reference to the territory east of Goshen in the northeastern corner of Egypt, rather than some unknown territory east of Canaan. Jeremiah suggests as much. He places the land of Uz between Egypt and Philistia:

"Pharaoh king of Egypt, and his servants, and his princes, and all his people;

"And all the mingled people, and all the kings of the land of Uz, and all the kings of the land of the Philistines, and Ashkelon, and Azzah [Gaza], and Ekron, and the remnant of Ashdod,

"Edom, and Moab, and the children of Ammon" (Jeremiah 25:19-21).

It is quite possible that biblical scholars simply overlooked Jeremiah's reference to the land of Uz being between Egypt and Philistia. Jeremiah starts out with Egypt, mentions Uz, then writes about the land of the Philistines, whose major cities were Ashkelon, Gaza, Ekron and Ashdod. Next he writes of Edom, Moab and Ammon in successive order from south to north. Jeremiah does not jump around with his geographical references. Therefore, it stands to reason that Jeremiah also mentioned Egypt, Uz and Philistia in correct order from south to north.

The reading of the passage leads one to conclude that Uz was located east of Goshen and may have extended across the southern border of Philistia — as far east as the territory of Edom. The book of Lamentations speaks of Edom dwelling in the land of Uz:

"Rejoice and be glad, O daughter of Edom, that dwellest in the land of Uz ..." (Lamentations 4:21).

It is possible that the land of Uz may have been the name of a wide region encompassing many tribes. Job, however, must have lived just east of the Nile delta. It is quite likely that Job was an Israelite, son of Issachar, and that he grew rich as a keeper of cattle — the very occupation of Jacob's family when they settled in Egypt. Just because Job was a man of position, whose wealth was measured in cattle and possessions, does not mean that he conformed to the picture of roving Chaldean tribesmen in the second millennium B.C.

Just because the Sabeans and Chaldeans robbed him does not mean that he had to live in the Arabian Desert, as some suggest. The Sabeans and Chaldeans traveled the trade routes between Babylon and Egypt regularly. Northeastern Egypt was right in the middle of the most heavily traveled caravan route extending from Mesopotamia through Egypt and into Africa.

Some think that the book has a strong Aramaic flavor and that Job lived near the center of Aramaic influence. During the second millennium B.C., Aramean tribes settled in the Fertile Crescent from the land of Babylonia to the rivers of Egypt and con-

trolled the caravan routes throughout the Middle East.
Evidently, Job lived along a major trade route for
these caravans.

When the Sabeans and Chaldeans robbed him, Job
did not pursue. Had he lived in the Mesopotamia
Valley, it would have been a simple matter for Job's
friends to round up the culprits. The fact that they
did not, suggests that they took the booty too far away
— too far for Job to muster an army and go after them.

So, When Was the Book Written?

The book of Job is considered to be the oldest book
in the Bible — predating Moses. Job must have lived
during the early part of those 230 years that the sons
of Jacob occupied the land of Goshen — along the
fertile delta of the Nile — having moved there at the
invitation of Joseph.

According to Genesis 36:15, Job's friend, Eliphaz,
and his son, Teman, were descendants of Esau, twin
brother to Jacob and progenitor of the Edomite
people. Geographically, Teman was an Edomite city.

*"These were the dukes of the sons of Esau: the sons of
Eliphaz the firstborn son of Esau; duke Teman, duke Omar,
duke Zepho, duke Kenaz,*

*"Duke Korah, duke Gatam, and duke Amalek: these are
the dukes that came of Eliphaz in the land of Edom ..."*
(Genesis 36:15,16).

Teman was the son of Eliphaz and grandson of
Esau. Furthermore, a city was named after him. According to Jeremiah 49:7, the city of Teman was once

considered to be a center of wisdom:

*"Concerning Edom, thus saith the LORD of hosts; Is wisdom no more in **Teman**? is counsel perished from the prudent? is their wisdom vanished?"* (Jeremiah 49:7).

It is also possible that the book was written some years after Job's death and during the period of suffering under Egyptian bondage. It may have been written as an inspiration for the Israelites to keep trusting in the God of their fathers in spite of their harsh circumstances. The story of Job gave hope to an otherwise hopeless people.

It is even possible that someone contemporary with Moses wrote the book — though we have no historical evidence. Whoever wrote this longest narrative of a single man in the Bible had to be quite gifted — an educated author with a flair for writing.

We are told that Job eventually regained his wealth and lived to see four generations:

"After this lived Job an hundred and forty years, and saw his sons, and his sons' sons, even four generations.
"So Job died, being old and full of days" (Job 42:16,17).

The term *"four generations"* has a familiar ring to it. That was the number of generations that God mentioned to Abraham when He predicted the Egyptian bondage:

"And he said unto Abram, Know of a surety that thy seed shall be a stranger in a land that is not theirs, and shall serve them; and they shall afflict them four hundred years;
"And also that nation, whom they shall serve, will I judge: and afterward shall they come out with great substance.

"And thou shalt go to thy fathers in peace; thou shalt be buried in a good old age.
"But in the fourth generation they shall come hither again: for the iniquity of the Amorites is not yet full" (Genesis 15:13-16).

We do not know the age of the Job in the Genesis account, when Issachar moved to Egypt, but he must have been quite young, since Joseph was only in his early thirties. Issachar, himself, could not have been much older than Joseph, being the ninth son of Jacob's twelve. If listed in the order of their ages, Job was the third son of Issachar, listed among four. So he may have been a child when the family moved to Egypt.

We are told that Job lived 140 years after his ordeal and died a rich man — perhaps some years before the onset of Pharaoh's persecution of the Chosen People. The story of Job's life could have been written as an encouragement for the Israelites who were suffering Egyptian bondage.

There is no mention of Egypt in the book of Job, but that could have been because the writer did not want to stir the waters of a delicate political situation. One may recall, when Moses interrupted Egypt's tranquility, Pharaoh's persecution of the Israelites took a distinct turn for the worse.

No one really knows when Job was written. But we cannot dismiss the possibility that Job appealed to a disheartened people facing the cruel antics of the Pharaoh who knew not Joseph. The Israelites were enslaved and made to work for the mad ruler.

The Prophetic Aspects of Job

Job is the story of a suffering man whose hope and destiny lay in the hands of God:

"There was a man in the land of Uz, whose name was Job; and that man was perfect and upright, and one that feared God, and eschewed evil.

"And there were born unto him seven sons and three daughters.

"His substance also was seven thousand sheep, and three thousand camels, and five hundred yoke of oxen, and five hundred she asses, and a very great household; so that this man was the greatest of all the men of the east" (Job 1:1-3).

The story of Job is basically this: Job was a man greatly blessed of God because of his righteousness. It seemed that God had a wall of protection around Job and had made him one of the richest men in the world. But the great accuser came before the throne of God and declared that, if given a chance, Job could be made to curse his Creator. Basically, that's when the persecution of Job began.

Job was not a vile and wicked man. His persecution was more than just a punishment for sin. As best we can determine, it was God's way of testing the ruggedness and durability of His Creation.

That is what men do today when a new product is developed. For example, the space shuttle has been through hundreds of rigorous trials in order to see whether it would stand the test. Once it passed all of the testing, then it was ready to perform the great task for which it was designed. Such is true of the human race and especially Israel, for God had promised Abraham that through his seed all of the families of the earth would be blessed.

There are some who believe that God has disinherited Israel and that New Testament Christianity has replaced the Chosen People as the heirs to the Covenant. Such is not the case, however, for we must remember that even though Job appeared to be forsaken, in the end he was restored and given a greater position than that which he possessed before his problems began. I am convinced that Job lays out a prophetic scenario for the nation of Israel.

Job lost everything he had. Satan had claimed that if an ill wind were allowed to blow upon the life of Job he would curse God. In response, the Lord allowed an army of Sabeans to slay his servants and steal his 500 yoke of oxen. At the same time a fire fell from heaven and destroyed his 7,000 sheep.

Furthermore, soon afterward, a band of Chaldeans stole his 3,000 camels. As if that were not enough, God also allowed a violent wind to destroy the house where his seven sons and three daughters were feasting. There were no survivors. Almost overnight Job lost everything.

The devastated Job then arose, tore his mantle, shaved his head, and fell upon the ground to say:

"... the LORD gave, and the LORD hath taken away; blessed be the name of the LORD .
"In all this Job sinned not, nor charged God foolishly"
(Job 1:21-22).

If that were not enough, God allowed Job to suffer a physical illness:

"So went Satan forth from the presence of the LORD, and smote Job with sore boils from the sole of his foot unto his crown" (Job 2:7).

Thoroughly demoralized, the pitiful Job took a piece of broken pottery with which to scrape his boils and sat down among some ashes. The ashes were probably prepared as a disinfectant and cleansing agent for the oozing sores that covered his body. Both Job and his wife were emotionally devastated, not only by their bankruptcy, but also by the loss of their children. Through it all, Job maintained his faith in God, but his wife could not:

"Then said his wife unto him, Dost thou still retain thine integrity? curse God, and die" (Job 2:9).

Job's wife is typical of that part of the family of Israel, which could not stand the test. The Israeli people have certainly had their share of testing.

It is said that during the days of World War II, in one of the concentration camps, some of the Jewish prisoners put God on trial. They had attorneys for the plaintiff and attorneys for the defendant. Court was convened, and for several days arguments were heard. The accusations were made that God was responsible for all of the problems that beset the Jews. After several days of deliberation, the jury brought in its verdict. They declared that God was guilty. Sounds like the wife of Job. "Give up," she said. "Curse God, and die."

I have heard it said that some Jews have prayed, "Oh, God, if we are the Chosen People, please choose somebody else for a while!" Such has been the dilemma of the Jew in the midst of a persecution greater than that which has befallen any other race or nationality throughout the annals of history.

Job's Three Friends

In the depths of his illness, Job's three friends came to comfort him — Eliphaz, the Temanite; Bildad, the Shuhite; and Zophar, the Naamathite.

Unfortunately, they were far from being a comfort to the hurting Job. Prophetically, may I suggest that these friends appear to represent the three basic divisions of the human race — the descendants of Shem, Ham, and Japheth — who, instead of being a comfort to the persecuted Israel down through the centuries, have taken the place of the accuser.

Eliphaz delivered three speeches, Bildad three and Zophar two. Following each discourse, Job defended himself. Basically, these three friends had one view of the problem — Job was a hypocrite. Though he appeared to be outwardly good, they believed him to be a wicked man. Otherwise, according to their concept of God, the suffering of Job would be unjust. Job, on the other hand, though he was suffering, would not accuse the justice of God. In chapter 9, verse 2, Job was faced with the frustrating question, *"... how should man be just with God?"*

In verses 32 and 33, he continued:

"For he is not a man, as I am, that I should answer him, and we should come together in judgment.

"Neither is there any daysman betwixt us, that might lay his hand upon us both" (Job 9:32,33).

What a dilemma! Job admits that he has no daysman — no advocate — no lawyer — to plead his case. In chapter 19, however, his faith was rewarded by the revelation of a coming Redeemer and by a future resurrection:

"For I know that my redeemer liveth, and that he shall stand at the latter day upon the earth:

"And though after my skin worms destroy this body, yet in my flesh shall I see God" (Job 19:25,26).

This observation made in the midst of his suffering represents a prophecy of the coming resurrection. It implies a magnificent promise of Christ, who will return someday to raise the dead and save Israel from its dilemma.

Eliphaz, Bildad, and Zophar believed Job was afflicted because of some great sin he had committed before God. However, there are many sinners in the world who do not suffer as Job suffered. Therefore, the suffering of Job cannot be attributed to some secret sin. Eliphaz, Bildad, and Zophar were also sinners before God, and yet they were not afflicted as Job was. Now, to be sure, the Chosen People have suffered because of sin, but there must be a far more important reason for the suffering of Israel.

The three friends of Job, which I believe represent the three divisions of the human race, seem to regard God as small and petty, exacting in His relations with men — basically that God only rewards good and punishes evil. They would look at anyone who is suffering and accuse him of deserving punishment. This appears to be a worldwide view of Jewish suffering. The world is quick to condemn the Jew.

Elihu, The Buzite

At this point in the story, another man made his appearance — Elihu, the son of Barachel, the Buzite. Elihu presented a more accurate opinion of the problem. His account of God is noble and true. It is noteworthy that in the last chapter, God did not classify him with the other three philosophers.

If Eliphaz, Bildad, and Zophar represent the three divisions of humanity, and if Job represents the nation of Israel, then who is Elihu and what does he represent? It is my opinion that Elihu represents Christianity's concept of God. The word Elihu means "God of him." The word Barachel means "God hath blessed." These words seem to be prophetically descriptive of New Testament Christianity.

On the other hand, Elihu was a Buzite, a term that means "scorned, despised." Unfortunately, this too is indicative of Christianity down through the centuries. Christianity has also been the brunt of criticism by an unbelieving world. The opinion of many today is that Christians are trying to shove religion down everybody's throat, and that ministers are only preaching for money. Yes, just like Elihu the Buzite, Christians are scorned and hated. As a prophetic type of Christianity, Elihu admitted that he was younger than Job and his three friends:

"And Elihu the son of Barachel the Buzite answered and said, I am young, and ye are very old; wherefore I was afraid, and durst not show you mine opinion" (Job 32:6).

Just as Elihu considered himself to be younger than the others, even so, Christianity is a relatively young religion — younger than Israel — younger than the human race. If Elihu is a prophetic profile of Christianity, then some of his opinions also reflect the opinions of Christianity. He said of Job and his three friends:

"...there was none of you that convinced Job, or that answered his words:
"Lest ye should say, We have found out wisdom: God thrusteth him down, not man" (Job 32:12-13).

Elihu perceived that they could not convince Job of his sin, nor could Job convince them of his innocence. Job's three friends refused to listen to Job's defense, for they would not admit that they could possibly be wrong. They considered Job to be suffering because he was a bad man. They did not want to believe that Job could be good.

Such is the world today. Most are not willing to give Israel the benefit of the doubt. On the other hand, Elihu accused Job of speaking words without wisdom and multiplying his words without knowledge:

"Job hath spoken without knowledge, and his words were without wisdom" (Job 34:35).

"Therefore doth Job open his mouth in vain; he multiplieth words without knowledge" (Job 35:16).

That was not nice of Elihu to accuse Job. When God appeared and began to speak, He accused Elihu of the same thing:

"Who is this that darkeneth counsel by words without knowledge?" (Job 38:2).

Elihu was guilty of the same indiscretion he leveled against Job. Such is true, I think, of Christianity. Let us not be so quick to condemn Israel, for we have no right to throw stones.

The appearance of the Lord seems to be a prophetic picture of the Second Coming of Jesus Christ in power and great glory:

"Then the LORD answered Job out of the whirlwind ..." (Job 38:1).

The *shekinah* glory on the day of Pentecost was described as a rushing mighty wind — *"tongues like as of fire"* (Acts 2:3) sat upon each of them. It is the same kind of appearance as was given on Mt. Sinai when God came down in the pillar of cloud and fire.

At the end of Job's affliction God came to make His judgment, and frankly He didn't have much good to say about Job, his three friends, or Elihu. And of Job He said, *"Where wast thou when I laid the foundations of the earth?"* (Job 38:4). And finally, of Eliphaz and his friends God said:

"My wrath is kindled against thee, and against thy two friends: for ye have not spoken of me the thing that is right, as my servant Job hath" (Job 42:7).

God's wrath kindled here, may be a prediction of Armageddon. Please note, disaster was averted when Job prayed for his friends. At this point, God turned the captivity of Job.

He either gave him seven more sons and three more daughters, or He raised his seven sons and three daughters from the dead and returned them to their father. At least it appears to be a prophecy of the future resurrection. Otherwise the Bible might have said that God gave seven MORE sons and three MORE daughters:

"He had also seven sons and three daughters" (Job 42:13).

Furthermore, the Lord blessed the latter end of Job more than his beginning and doubled his riches. So, who was Job? He was the ultimate Jew. He was a prophetic profile of the Chosen People in their suffering and their destiny. We can be certain that God will turn the captivity of Israel just as He turned the captivity of Job.

Chapter Six

The Story of Joshua

"Joshua fit the battle of Jericho, and the walls came tumblin' down." We're all familiar with that lively old spiritual. But there is more to the life of Joshua than just the Battle of Jericho. In fact, the life of Joshua was a prophecy. His life offers one of the great prophetic types of the First and Second Advents of Jesus Christ. Though Moses led the children of Israel out of Egyptian bondage, it was Joshua who led them into the Promised Land. Toward the end of his ministry, Moses made a prediction:

"The LORD thy God will raise up unto thee a Prophet from the midst of thee, of thy brethren, like unto me; unto him ye shall harken" (Deuteronomy 18:15).

Though that prophecy was to be ultimately fulfilled in Jesus Christ, it also had an earlier fulfillment in Joshua, who succeeded Moses as leader of the children of Israel.

The very name of Joshua provides a prophecy of Jesus Christ. In the Hebrew language his name is pronounced Yeh-ho-shoo'-ah, meaning "Jehovah Savior." That same Hebrew word is translated in our New Testament as Jesus. It is basically the same name.

God, in choosing Joshua to succeed Moses, was literally giving a prophecy of the future name of His Son, "Jehovah Savior." His name is *"above every name"* (Phil 2:9), for there is *"none other name under heaven given among men, whereby we must be saved"* (Acts 4:12). And at the name of Jesus, one day *"every knee shall bow ... and every tongue shall confess"* (Romans 14:11) that Jesus is Lord, to the glory of God the Father. That is why the angel said unto Mary, *"that holy thing which shall be born of thee shall be called the Son of God."* (Luke 1:35). Truly, Jesus is our Yeh-ho-shoo'-ah, "Jehovah Savior."

The War with Amalek

The first time Joshua appeared in the Bible, he was given command of Israel's army in a battle against Amalek. The event occurred at the beginning of the 40 year wilderness journey and is found in Exodus 17:8-13. That battle was the first in a series of wars which culminated in the taking of the Promised Land some 40 years later. Each of those wars, by the way, seem to represent a prophetic picture of the Arab-Israeli wars of this generation.

Descending Sinai

The next time Joshua appeared was at Sinai when Moses went up into the mountain to receive the oracles of God. According to the Scripture, Joshua accompanied Moses up the mountain (Exodus 24:13). Forty days later when Moses brought the two tables of stone down from the summit, Joshua was with him (Exodus 32:15-17).

This is a prophetic picture of the First Advent of Jesus Christ. Though Moses represented the main picture of the Messiah, we nevertheless are reminded that Joshua accompanied him at this point. The two men together offer a prophetic picture of both the Deity and the humanity of Christ — Moses, having been in the presence of God, offers a picture of His Deity and Joshua reveals His humanity.

The Tabernacle of the Congregation

When they got to the foot of the mountain, they found that the people had built a golden calf. Moses, representing the Deity of Christ, became angry and broke the tables of stone. It is said that he took down his own tent, hauled it outside the camp of Israel, and set it up. He called the elders of the people together and, pointing to his tent, and called it *"the Tabernacle of the congregation."* (Exodus 33:7).

Joshua accompanied Moses into the tent. The Glory of God descended at the door and God spoke to Moses *"face to face"* (v. 11). When the cloud was lifted, Moses left the tent, but Joshua stayed inside!

This is a prophetic picture of the First Advent of Jesus Christ. When the Savior came the first time, He found the Chosen People steeped in unbelief. In a manner of speaking, Jesus left the congregation of Israel and established His dwelling place outside the camp. We call it the New Testament Church. That tent of Moses was a prophetic picture of New Testament Christianity which was to be established outside the camp of Israel.

When Moses left the tent, Joshua stayed inside giving a prophetic picture of Jesus Christ, who has remained outside the camp of Israel for these past 2,000 years and inside the *"tabernacle of the congregation"* — namely the New Testament Church. It is to us that Jesus gave the promise, *"Lo, I am with you alway, even unto the end of the world."* (Matthew 28:20).

Kadesh-barnea

The next prophetic picture of Joshua can be found at Kadesh-barnea. Joshua was among the twelve spies who were sent into the Promised Land to bring back a report. Joshua, along with Caleb, brought back a good report. They urged the people to make immediate plans to take the Promised Land. However, the other ten spies brought back a negative report. They were fearful of the giants and were not at all confident that they could conquer the country.

At this point the hearts of the people melted. They rejected the testimony of Joshua and refused to enter the Promised Land.

In like manner, when Jesus came the first time, His message was rejected by the Jewish people. They, too, refused His offer of the promised kingdom of heaven. *"He came unto His own, and His own received Him not"* (John 1:11). The message of our Savior was not believed, and just as Israel spent the next 40 years wandering in the wilderness, even so the Jewish people have spent these past 2,000 years wandering in the wilderness of this world among the Gentile nations. History has called them "the Wandering Jew."

Perhaps those 40 years in the wilderness represent a prophecy in times, for there are 40 jubilees in the course of 2,000 years. If those 40 years in the wilderness prophetically represent 40 jubilees, then let us pose the question: is it possible that Christ could soon return to celebrate the beginning of a new era — the millennial reign of Christ?

Forty Years Later

At this point in the story, Joshua fades from view. He is not heard from again until the 40 years are completed. The next time we see Joshua, Moses has been instructed to transfer the leadership of the children of Israel to him (Numbers 27:15-23). This is a prophetic picture of the Second Coming of Christ, and it is interesting to note that the spirit which rested upon Moses was transferred to Joshua.

After the death of Moses, Joshua became the leader of Israel. He was given the task of leading his people across the Jordan into the Promised Land. In like manner, Jesus Christ will return one day to establish yet another Promised Land — the millennial kingdom.

The Early Wars

The events which followed in the life of Joshua, namely the conquest of Canaan, offer a magnificent prophetic picture of those events which shall occur in the last generation. Even the wars seem to present a prophetic picture of those future wars leading up to the awesome Battle of Armageddon. For instance, the battle against Amalek, at the beginning of the 40 year journey, seems to point to the 1948 Arab-Israeli War.

The battle against Og and Sihon seems to represent the 1956 Arab-Israeli War, and the taking of Jericho could be a prophetic picture of the 1967 Six-Day War, when the Jewish people once again took that same territory, called today the West Bank. The Battle of Jericho took one week. In like manner, the 1967 war has been called an historic Six-Day War. It, too, took just one week. The 1967 Six-Day War is regarded as a miracle war.

The next battle fought by Joshua and the children of Israel was a near disaster. It occurred at the city of Ai and could be a prophetic picture of the 1973 Yom Kippur War which, likewise, was a near disaster for the Jewish people.

In the story, the army of Israel almost lost the battle because there was sin in the camp. Achan had taken a goodly Babylonian garment and a wedge of gold. In like manner, the nation of Israel almost lost the Yom Kippur War. The little nation lost 3,000 of its finest young men in 1973. Three and one-half years later, it was found out that Yitzhak Rabin, the prime minister of Israel, had a foreign bank account in Washington, D. C. Since it was against Israeli law, he had to resign in disgrace — shades of Achan and his wedge of gold.

The Peace Treaty with Gibeon

After the Battle of Ai the men of Gibeon played a trick on the Chosen People. They sent a group of representatives to the Israelite camp to negotiate a peace treaty. They dressed in old clothes and well-worn shoes to give the appearance that they had traveled from a far distance in order to make peace with the Jews.

According to the Scripture, the elders of Israel agreed to the peace accord. Joshua 9:14 recorded that the elders of Israel did not ask the counsel of the Lord when they made the treaty. Later, they found out that they had been tricked by the Gibeonites.

Nevertheless, they still agreed to keep the provisions of the treaty. This created a furor among the tribes and *"... all the congregation murmured against the princes."* (Joshua 9:18). Could Israel be repeating that mistake by making treaties with Egypt, Jordan, and the PLO?

Anwar Sadat came to Jerusalem in November of 1977, with an offer of peace. In the months that followed, Menachem Begin and Anwar Sadat agreed upon the Camp David Accord and signed the peace treaty in March of 1979, on the White House lawn. President Jimmy Carter witnessed the signing of that historic document.

Under the provisions of that treaty the Sinai was returned to Egypt. However, some Israeli people felt they had been tricked. A great furor broke out among the people, and over a million Israeli citizens signed a petition to try to keep the government from returning the Sinai. Thousands of dissidents swarmed the Sinai and had to be forcibly removed.

According to the story given in the book of Joshua, the men of Gibeon were attacked by their neighboring kingdoms because they had negotiated a peace treaty with Israel. In like manner, Egypt has been assailed by its Arab neighbors for negotiating its peace with the Jews. We can say that Egypt was smitten. Anwar Sadat was killed.

If the Gibeonite treaty is a prophetic picture of the Egyptian-Israeli treaty, then we should expect a continual deteriorating situation in the Middle East that will ultimately bring on that last series of battles which will devastate the earth and culminate in the Second Coming of Christ.

Since the treaty with Egypt, Israel has routed out

the PLO in Lebanon (1981-82), faced the Palestinian Intifada (1987-93), negotiated a treaty with Arafat in 1993 and Jordan in 1994. Hamas terrorists still haunt the tiny nation and Hezbollah troops continue to shell Northern Israel with Katyusha rockets.

It is my opinion that a series of wars will involve at least three future major battles: the "Battle of Gog and Magog," the "Abomination of Desolation," and the awesome "Armageddon."

As a result of Joshua's ancient treaty, five neighboring kingdoms made war against the Gibeonites. Under the onslaught of those neighboring kingdoms, the men of Gibeon sent a message of distress to Joshua. "Come quickly," they said, "for we are under attack."

According to the Scripture, Joshua and the army of Israel came to the aid of the Gibeonites. They were successful in routing out the enemy and pursued them along the way to Beth-horon:

"And it came to pass, as they fled from before Israel, and were in the going down to Beth-horon, that the LORD cast down great stones from heaven upon them unto Azekah, and they died: they were more which died with hailstones than they whom the children of Israel slew with the sword.

"Then spake Joshua to the LORD in the day when the LORD delivered up the Amorites before the children of Israel, and he said in the sight of Israel, Sun, stand thou still upon Gibeon; and thou, Moon, in the valley of Ajalon.

"And the sun stood still, and the moon stayed, until the people had avenged themselves upon their enemies. Is not

this written in the book of Jasher? So the sun stood still in the midst of heaven, and hasted not to go down about a whole day" (Joshua 10:11-13).

What a magnificent picture of the Tribulation Period! According to Revelation 16:21, great hailstones will once again plague the enemies of Israel! Furthermore, it was in that great battle that Joshua ordered the sun to stand still over Gibeon and the moon to remain over Ajalon.

It is a prophetic picture of that great day when the future Joshua, Jesus Christ, will come to fight the prophetic Battle of Armageddon. At His command the sun and the moon will be affected. The sun will turn as black as sackcloth of ashes, and the moon will turn as blood — fulfilling the prophecy of that day when Joshua made the sun stand still.

Setting Up the Kingdom

After Joshua and the armies of Israel conquered Canaan, they set about to divide it among the Twelve Tribes. This may be a prophetic picture of that which shall occur at the beginning of the millennial reign of Christ. Those who have been faithful to the Savior will be given positions of leadership.

Remember the story of the talents in Matthew 25? One servant was made to be ruler over ten cities, and another was made to be ruler over four cities — each according to his faithfulness. This is basically the same thing that is pictured in the book of Joshua.

Caleb Remained Faithful

Remember Caleb? He was one of the twelve spies who had entered the Promised Land with Joshua from the Israelite camp at Kadesh Barnea. He and Joshua were the only two among the twelve spies who were confident that God had given them the Land.

Caleb came to Joshua in chapter 14, verse 6, and reminded him that he too had believed some 45 years before. While the other ten spies had complained that Israel appeared as grasshoppers in the sight of the giants, Joshua and Caleb remained faithful. Because of unbelief, Israel spent 40 years wandering in the wilderness. And now Caleb, 85 years old, asked for the very mountain where the giants were located. He wanted to prove to Israel that their fears had been groundless. Caleb drove out the giants and received the mountain stronghold of Hebron for his own family inheritance.

Question: Who does Caleb prophetically represent in the story? Well, it appears that Caleb was a Gentile. His father, Jephunneh, was a Kenezite of the tribe of Jethro, the father-in-law of Moses. Though he represented the tribe of Judah, he was a Gentile — related to the Gentile bride of Moses!

I believe Caleb represents Gentile Christianity who, in the first century, tried to convince the Jews that their long-awaited kingdom was immediately available. However, because of their unbelief, the kingdom must await another wilderness journey — the spiritual journey of these past 2,000 years.

Just before the children of Israel crossed the Jordan River and set up their base camp at Gilgal, Joshua spoke to the tribes of Reuben and Gad and half the tribe of Manasseh who wanted to stay on the east side of the Jordan and establish their cities.

Joshua warned them to stay faithful to the goals of the Israelite nation and to help fight for the rest of the land until all of it was conquered:

"Remember the word which Moses the servant of the LORD commanded you, saying, The LORD your God hath given you rest, and hath given you this land.

"Your wives, your little ones, and your cattle, shall remain in the land which Moses gave you on this side of Jordan; but ye shall pass before your brethren armed, all the mighty men of valor, and help them;

"Until the LORD have given your brethren rest, as he hath given you, and they also have possessed the land which the LORD your God giveth them: then ye shall return unto the land of your possession, and enjoy it, which Moses the LORD'S servant gave you on this side Jordan toward the sunrising.

"And they answered Joshua, saying, All that thou commandest us we will do, and whithersoever thou sendest us, we will go" (Joshua 1:13-16).

This concurs with an earlier warning given by Moses in Numbers 32:23 when he said, *"... be sure your sin will find you out."* This famous passage deals with those Jews who, after conquering their little bit of land, wanted to quit the battle and not help the others gain their inheritance. Perhaps that is a pro-phetic picture of today's generation of Jews, for even though there are some 14 million Jews in the world, only four million of them have gone back to the Promised Land.

Israel's establishment of the Messianic Kingdom is in the making today — as a fulfillment of the prophetic life of Joshua, a type of the First and Second Advents of Jesus Christ.

Chapter Seven

Caleb, the Gentile

Two years after the Exodus, Israel camped at Kadesh-barnea on the southern border of the Promised Land. Moses chose twelve men to scout the land of Canaan and bring back a report. Twelve men were chosen to represent the Twelve Tribes of Israel.

Those twelve men spent forty days on a reconnaissance mission and returned with their reports. Ten of the men brought back a negative report. They claimed there were giants in the land and that the Israelites were *"in our own sight as grasshoppers, and so we were in their sight"* (Numbers 13:33). Two of the spies, however, brought back a challenge for the Jewish people to enter immediately and possess the kingdom. Unfortunately, the majority refused to believe their message and rejected their challenge.

Because of their unbelief, the children of Israel had to wander forty years in the wilderness before they were allowed to enter the Promised Land. During that time, the people over twenty years of age died in the wilderness. They were not allowed to possess the kingdom. Only Joshua and Caleb survived. The other ten spies died of a plague.

We learned in the previous chapter that Joshua succeeded Moses and led the children of Israel across the Jordan River. He guided them to victory in the battle for Jericho. Also, he was noted for making the sun stand still over the Valley of Beth-horon near the town of Gibeon. Therefore, Joshua is a prophetic type of Christ.

Caleb is another important figure. He and Joshua were the only two spies who had given a good report at the beginning of their sojourn in the wilderness. Though Joshua represented the tribe of Ephraim, Caleb represented the tribe of Judah. Both Joshua and Caleb are important in Jewish history.

In the second century of the Christian era the rabbis wrote about two messiahs. One they called "Messiah Ben-Joseph" (the son of Joseph) and "Messiah Ben-David" (the son of David). The early rabbis respected both Joseph and David for their great contributions to Jewish heritage.

One may assume they wrote about Messiah Ben-Joseph because Ephraim was the son of Joseph, and the Joshua was chosen to represent the tribe of

Ephraim. Likewise, they wrote about Messiah Ben-David because David was of the tribe of Judah, and Caleb was chosen to represent the tribe of Judah. The two long-looked-for messiahs correspond to Joshua and Caleb, who had encouraged the people to have the courage to possess the kingdom.

Caleb Was a Gentile

If Joshua is a type of Jesus, then who is Caleb, and what does he represent in God's prophetic plan? It appears that Caleb was a Gentile. His father, Jephunneh, was a Kenezite of the tribe of Jethro, the father-in-law of Moses. Though he represented the tribe of Judah, he was a Gentile — related to the wife of Moses!

"Then the children of Judah came unto Joshua in Gilgal: and Caleb the son of Jephunneh the Kenezite said unto him, Thou knowest the thing that the LORD said unto Moses the man of God concerning me and thee in Kadesh-barnea" (Joshua 14:6).

In these verses Caleb reminds Joshua of what happened forty-five years before. The other ten spies had compared the people to grasshoppers. Now, the eighty-five year-old Caleb comes to Joshua requesting the privilege of fighting the giants.

"Now therefore give me this mountain, whereof the LORD spake in that day; for thou heardest in that day how the Anakims were there, and that the cities were great and fenced: if so be the LORD will be with me, then I shall be able to drive them out, as the LORD said.

"And Joshua blessed him, and gave unto Caleb the son of Jephunneh Hebron for an inheritance.

"Hebron therefore became the inheritance of Caleb the son of Jephunneh the Kenezite unto this day, because that he wholly followed the LORD God of Israel" (Joshua 14:12-14).

Joshua gave Caleb the mountain where the giants lived. Caleb was given the privilege of routing out the giants. There are numerous prophecies derived from these Scriptures.

According to the *Zondervan Pictorial Encyclopedia of the Bible*, (Vol. 1, pg. 686), "Caleb's relationship with the Kenezites indicates the presence of non-Israelites who became identified with the people and faith of Israel."

Here is a Gentile chosen to represent the tribe of Judah — the leading tribe of Israel — the tribe from which the Messiah would come. Why was a Gentile chosen to represent the tribe of Judah? Perhaps because Judah had committed the scarlet sin with Tamar, his daughter-in-law, and from their unholy union came the illegitimate son, Pharez, in violation of the Law of God.

According to the Mosaic Law, no illegitimate son was allowed to enter into the congregation of the Lord until the tenth generation.

"A bastard shall not enter into the congregation of the LORD; even to his tenth generation shall he not enter into the congregation of the LORD" (Deuteronomy 23:2).

Because of the illegitimate son of Judah, a Gentile had to be chosen to represent the tribe. In fact, David was the tenth generation from the offspring of Judah. No one from the tribe of Judah was allowed a position in the congregation of the Lord until David, the tenth generation.

Hebron became the inheritance of Caleb, the son of Jephunneh the Kenezite *"... because that he wholly followed the LORD God of Israel"* (Joshua 14:14).

Who Does Caleb Represent?

Obviously, Caleb must be a prophetic picture of Gentile Christianity. The name Caleb means "dog" — a common term used when referring to Gentiles. Caleb, the Gentile dog, had become identified with the tribe of Judah — the same tribe from which our Savior came. In like manner, Gentile Christianity has become identified with the great offspring of the tribe of Judah, Jesus Christ, the Son of God.

Furthermore, just as Caleb was a relative of the Gentile bride of Moses, New Testament Christianity is identified as the Gentile bride of Christ. Both Moses and Joshua were prophetic types of Christ — the one representing the Deity of Christ and the other representing His humanity. Therefore, Gentile Christianity was pictured by Caleb, a substitute or stand-in for the tribe of Judah.

Caleb's Request

After Joshua conquers Canaan land, the 85 year old Caleb approaches him with a special request. He asks Joshua to let him fight the giants. Here is a prophetic picture of Armageddon. In the Bible, giants appear to represent the last great war of history — the giant of all wars — that awesome Armageddon.

Arba Means "Four"

Before the mountain was called Hebron, it was named Kirjath-arba — the city of Arba.

"And the name of Hebron before was Kirjath-arba; which Arba was a great man among the Anakims ..." (Joshua 14:15).

Please note the name of the mountain where the giants lived. The word Kirjath is an Old Testament term for city. Arba represents the name of the giant.

Arba means "four" — a mystical number representing the world. For instance, there were four columns in the Tabernacle which held up the blue veil separating the Holy Place (representing the dispensation of *Grace*) from the Holy of Holies (representing the Millennial Reign of Christ).

According to E. W. Bullinger, in his book *Number in Scripture*, those four columns represent the number of the world. They represent that day when the throne of God will be established upon the earth. Bullinger wrote:

"The number four is made up of three and one, and it denotes, therefore, that which follows the revelation of God in the Trinity — namely, His creative works. He is known by the things which are seen; hence, the written revelation commences with the words, *'In the beginning, God created ...'* Creation, is, therefore, the next thing, the fourth thing, and the number four always has reference to all that is created. It is the number of material completeness. Hence, it is the world number.

"Four is the number of the great elements: earth, air, fire, and water. Four are the regions of the earth: north, south, east, and west. Four are the divisions of the day: morning, noon, evening, and midnight. Four are the seasons of the year: spring, summer, autumn, and winter."

There was a special reason why four columns held up the veil in the Tabernacle that separated the Holy Place from the Holy of Holies. Let us say, by way of example, that they represent the four corners of the earth, and the beautiful blue veil in the Tabernacle represents the four winds of heaven — that blue, oxygen atmosphere that surrounds the world.

Just as the veil in the Temple was ripped from top to bottom on the day of our Savior's crucifixion, one day, at Armageddon, the real veil — the blue atmosphere — will be rolled back like a scroll, and our great High Priest shall emerge from the Holy of Holies of heaven to establish the throne of God upon the earth.

In Revelation 7:1-3, the Apostle John described the four columns along with the veil in this manner:

"And after these things I saw four angels standing on the four corners of the earth, holding the four winds of the earth, that the wind should not blow on the earth, nor on the sea, nor on any tree.

"And I saw another angel ascending from the east, having the seal of the living God: and he cried with a loud voice to the four angels, to whom it was given to hurt the earth and the sea,

"Saying, Hurt not the earth, neither the sea, nor the trees, till we have sealed the servants of our God in their foreheads" (Revelation 7:1-3).

These verses refer to the beginning of the Tribulation Period and to the sealing of 144,000 Jews for their special ministry during those seven years.

The description of four angels standing upon the four corners of the earth, holding the four winds of the earth, appears to be a fulfillment of the cherubim woven into the blue veil of the Tabernacle.

"And thou shalt make a veil of blue, and purple, and scarlet, and fine twined linen of cunning work: with cherubims shall it be made:

"And thou shalt hang it upon four pillars of shittim wood overlaid with gold: their hooks shall be of gold, upon the four sockets of silver.

"And thou shalt hang up the veil under the taches, that thou mayest bring in thither within the veil the ark of the testimony: and the veil shall divide unto you between the holy place and the most holy" (Exodus 26:31-33).

Those four columns, which supported the veil, prophetically represent events which will attend the conclusion of the dispensation of *Grace* and the beginning of the thousand-year reign of Christ. It is quite significant, then, that Caleb was allowed to fight the giants at Kirjath-arba, the "city of the four."

Arba Became Hebron

After Caleb conquered the mountain, the name was changed to Hebron. The name Hebron means "the seat of association." Please note: Caleb, the Gentile dog, came with the request, "I want that mountain." He is a type of Gentile Christianity which one day will possess the "seat of association" — namely the *"mountain of the LORD"* (Isa. 2:3).

Hebron was associated with Jerusalem. In fact, the city of Hebron became the first capital of Israel. King David ruled in Hebron for seven years before moving his throne to Jerusalem. Therefore, Hebron is the seat of association; it is associated with Jerusalem. In like manner, the heavenly Jerusalem is associated with the earthly Jerusalem. One day we will possess that great city, New Jerusalem.

The New Jerusalem is described in two places in the Bible as a great mountain — the mountain of the Lord. The first is found in Isaiah 2:2,3:

"And it shall come to pass in the last days, that the mountain of the LORD's house shall be established in the top of the mountains, and shall be exalted above the hills; and all nations shall flow unto it."

"And many people shall go and say, Come ye, and let us go up to the mountain of the LORD ..." (Isaiah 2:2,3).

The *"mountain of the Lord"* referred to in these verses represents the glorious Holy City, New Jerusalem.

"And I saw a new heaven and a new earth: for the first heaven and the first earth were passed away; and there was no more sea."

"And I John saw the holy city, new Jerusalem, coming down from God out of heaven, prepared as a bride adorned for her husband" (Revelation 21:1,2).

How do we know that the Holy City, New Jerusalem, is in the shape of a mountain? How do we know the mountain of the Lord is called the New Jerusalem? — by John's description in verses 9 and 10:

"And there came unto me one of the seven angels which had the seven vials full of the seven last plagues, and talked with me, saying, Come hither, I will show thee the bride, the Lamb's wife.

"And he carried me away in the spirit to a great and high mountain, and showed me that great city, the holy Jerusalem, descending out of heaven from God ..." (Revelation 21:9,10).

Please note: the angel carried John away to a great and high mountain. That great and high mountain was the Holy City, New Jerusalem.

Therefore, when Caleb said to Joshua, "I want that mountain," he was uttering a great, prophetic prediction. One day all the Caleb's of the world, namely New Testament Christianity, will inherit that "seat of association," that great *"mountain of the Lord"* — the Holy City, New Jerusalem.

So there you have it. In the story of Caleb, we can see a magnificent type of a vast throng of Gentiles who have become identified with the tribe of Judah. One day soon, we will come with Christ in power and great glory to fight the giant of Armageddon and to possess the *"mountain of the Lord."*

Chapter Eight

Ruth, The Gentile Bride

The story of Ruth is one of the most beautiful among the pages of the Bible. It is a classic love story, pulling at the heart strings of human emotion. More than that, the beloved Ruth was a prophetic type of New Testament Christianity. Being a Gentile bride, she married the kinsman redeemer — the wealthy Boaz, who was asked to redeem the land which once belonged to Naomi. As a prophetic type of Christ, Boaz welcomed the opportunity to restore the property.

Naomi was typical of Israel, who lost her land and lived among Gentiles. In the end, however, Naomi was returned to her land and Ruth was privileged to marry Boaz. With her marriage to the kinsman redeemer, Ruth received the greater inheritance.

First, the story — which occurred during the years of the transition from the judges to the monarchy. Eli was the ruling high priest in Israel during those years after Samson's death. Elimelech took his wife, Naomi, and their two children, Mahlon and Chilion, into the country of Moab to live.

Elimelech had lived in Bethlehem. He was of the royal house of Judah. Evidently, Elimelech was hurting financially during the famine. He lost his land and was forced to move. It must have been a sad and difficult day for Elimelech when he lost his property, but he was typical of Israel who also suffered over the centuries, as they fell to one invading force after another.

There was the Assyrian captivity of the northern ten tribes in 721 B.C. and the Babylonian captivity of the southern two tribes in 606 B.C. There was the Greek occupation under Alexander the Great in 323 B.C., the Syrian occupation under Antiochus Epiphanes in 168 B.C., and the Roman occupation which began with the invasion by Pompey in 63 B.C.

The Roman occupation was met with resistance — leading to the destruction of the Temple in A.D. 70 and the great "diaspora" after the Bar Kochba revolt in A.D. 135. The Jewish people were driven from their country and scattered among the Gentile nations. For the next 1,813 years, the Jewish people were exiled from their homeland.

At this point, let us take note of the characters which make up the story in the book of Ruth. First, there was Elimelech, whose name means "my God is King." He and his family lived in Bethlehem, which means "house of bread and praise." Please note, in the house of bread there was no bread. A famine had fallen across the land.

Prophetically, the land was a Promised Land — flowing with milk and honey — a land where God was King. Many years later, however, when the King arrived, He was rejected and nailed to a cross.

The word Naomi means "pleasant or happy." Such was to be the nation of Israel — the wife of Jehovah. However, after ten years among the Gentiles, Naomi returned to Bethlehem without her husband, without her children and without her possessions.

When she returned, she asked to be called Marah, which means "sorrow or bitterness." She is a prophetic type of the nation of Israel who returned to their land in 1948 after the bitter experiences of two millennia, including Hitler's Holocaust.

Furthermore, those years of exile can be described by the names of the two children born to Elimelech and Naomi. The word Mahlon means "sick" and the word Chilion means "pining." Day after day, throughout those years of exile, Naomi faced the sorrow and the hurting of the sick room.

Perhaps Mahlon was an invalid and Chilion, his brother, continually bore an attitude of pining — never happy, never playful. Day after day their hearts were heavy with one problem after another.

Such has been the nation of Israel over the past twenty centuries. The exiled Israelite people have found little time for relief and pleasure during those years of suffering. No wonder the pleasant Naomi changed her name to the bitterness of Marah when she finally returned to her native Bethlehem.

During those years in Moab, the two sons, called "sickness" and "pining," took Gentile brides. Mahlon married Ruth, whose name comes from an ancient root word meaning "companion, friendship, or beauty." To Chilion was given Orpah, which means "stiffnecked." Evidently, she was not a pleasant person. These names are descriptive of Israel during its exile.

Ruth was a good companion to her sickly husband, Mahlon. Orpah was like a millstone hung around the neck of Chilion. Ruth is a picture of true Christianity, which was brought into the family of God by the Jewish people and has been, over the past 2,000 years, a true friend of Israel.

Orpah, on the other hand, prophetically portrays another group of Gentiles who have not been quite so kind to Israel. Orpah represents that other great religion which found its roots in Judaism. It is my opinion that the Moslem world would have to be characterized as an Orpah — a stiffnecked people adamant against the Jews.

In the story, Naomi lost her husband and her children in the distant land. Furthermore, her sons died without producing any children of their own. We must admit that the Jews, though zealous in their religion, have never borne much spiritual fruit. All they have to show for those years in exile are two Gentile religious ideologies — that of Christianity and Islam.

According to the story, the day came, after ten years in Moab, when Naomi decided to return to her land. We can follow the prophetic scenario with the return of the Jewish people to the land of Israel in this century. When Naomi was ready to return she tried to disassociate herself from Ruth and Orpah.

It is a picture of the Jewish people who, in their bitterness, have tried to disassociate themselves from Christianity and Islam. One can hardly blame them, for Israel had no reason to be proud of its spiritual offspring.

At this point in the story, Orpah, the "stiffnecked," left Naomi and returned to live among the Moabites, who were enemies of Israel. There, I think, stands the world of Islam, which has associated itself with the enemies of Israel. Today, there is a continual contention between the two groups.

On the other hand, Ruth determined to be a companion and friend to Naomi who, in her bitterness, had changed her name to Marah. Upon her return, she had wanted nothing to do with Ruth. She begged her to stay behind, but Ruth countered with an eloquent and revealing compassion:

"Entreat me not to leave thee, or to return from following after thee: for whither thou goest, I will go; and where thou lodgest, I will lodge: thy people shall be my people, and thy God my God:

"Where thou diest, will I die, and there will I be buried: the LORD do so to me, and more also, if aught but death part thee and me" (Ruth 1:16,17).

Such is the attitude of true Christianity today. Our loyalty lies with Israel. Our respect for the Jewish people remains undaunted. We shall not forget that our Savior is a Jew and that the twelve disciples who carried out His great commission were Jews. We shall not forget that the God of Israel is our God.

According to the *Midrash*, the historical writings of the Jewish people, Ruth was the daughter of Aglon, king of Moab — a princess of royal lineage. She was not just a common Moabite girl. Therefore, let us follow Ruth with great interest and see what part she played in the return of Naomi to her land.

This return was fulfilled in our generation. It began just before the turn of the century in the late 1890s, when Theodore Hertzel began to prepare his people for their return. The taking of Jerusalem in 1917 was another step in the fulfillment of the prophecy. A great milestone was marked when the nation was born in 1948. Naomi is home again! Oh, she may be bitter, but at least she's back in her land.

Now let us get to the best part of the story. When Naomi and Ruth returned to Bethlehem, Ruth set about to take care of the aged Naomi. Ruth was a princess, yet, she was willing to become a common laborer among the harvest fields of Bethlehem.

Her main desire was to provide for Naomi. What love she must have had! She was no ordinary person. What a more fitting place could there be for Ruth to work than among the harvest fields. As a type of New Testament Christianity, we have been busy among the harvest fields of this world, over the centuries, carrying out the admonition of our Savior to:

"Lift up your eyes, and look on the fields; for they are white already to harvest" (John 4:35).

Where was Naomi during this time? She was not to be found among the harvest fields. As a type of Israel, we must say that Judaism has been a rather exclusive religion down through the centuries. They have not been busy trying to win the world to the one true God.

At this point, Boaz enters the picture. He saw the beautiful Ruth gathering the grain in his field and his heart went out to her. He even set about to make her work easier. He told the young men who worked among the fields ahead of Ruth to leave "handfuls of purpose" (Ruth 2:16), that her work load might be easier and that her harvest might be greater. When Ruth came home that evening bringing an abundance of grain, Naomi immediately recognized the affection her kinsman had displayed for her.

At this point, Naomi still did not have her land. Oh, she was back home, but she was not in possession of her husband's inheritance. In like manner, the Jewish people are back in the land of Israel today, but their possession is not yet secure. A great controversy still rages in the Middle East over the presence of the Jews in the land. Obviously, the land will not be fully returned until the great Kinsman Redeemer comes to redeem it.

Naomi, with her keenness of mind, devised a plan whereby the beautiful Ruth could approach the wealthy Boaz and plead Naomi's case. She did this when she went to the threshing floor that night to lay at his feet.

According to the Scripture, it was at the end of the barley harvest that Ruth approached the kinsman redeemer. That places it in late May or early June around the festival of Pentecost. In fact, the book of Ruth is read every year in synagogues around the world during Pentecost. How fitting! Pentecost marked the entrance of Gentile Christianity. The coming of the Holy Spirit gave power to the early church for its great ministry among the harvest fields of the world.

According to ancient rabbinical teaching, Boaz had been married before, but his wife had died. In fact, he had just buried his first wife shortly before Ruth entered his harvest fields. Now, I do not know if there is a prophetic significance attached to that part of his life, for it is not recorded in the pages of the Bible. All we are told is that Boaz was eligible and that he fell in love with Ruth. But in passing, let me say that it is possible that the deceased wife of Boaz possessed certain characteristics to Old Testament Judaism, who was considered among the prophets of the Old Testament to be the adulterous wife of Jehovah.

When Ruth came to lay at his feet, Boaz was delighted. He was comforted in his sorrow. He had found the opportunity for happiness and fruitfulness. In the story, Boaz gave to Ruth six measures of barley and sent her back to Naomi. Those six measures of barley represented six days of work.

"... go not empty unto thy mother-in-law" (Ruth 3:17).

In a prophetic sense, those six measures of barley may represent six thousand years of human history, for after six days there comes the Sabbath rest. I think Boaz was saying to Ruth that the time had come for her to rest. She had labored enough. Her marriage was soon to take place. It is a beautiful picture of the great Sabbath, when we, who are the bride of Christ, will consummate our marriage to Him. We shall rule and reign with Him for a thousand years.

Before the wealthy Boaz could redeem Naomi's land and marry the beautiful Ruth, he had to clear it with the next of kin, for there was another kinsman who, by Law, had the right of first choice. In chapter four of the book, Boaz went up to the gate of the city, gathered ten witnesses and approached the nearer kinsman.

When Boaz asked him to redeem the land for Naomi, the nearer kinsman was willing to do it. However, when Boaz asked him if he was willing to marry Ruth, the nearer kinsman declined. He said, it might mar his own inheritance. This is just what Boaz had hoped to hear. It cleared the way for him to marry Ruth.

According to the Jewish historian, Flavius Josephus, Ruth was present at the meeting and, according to the Law, Josephus said that Ruth took the shoe from the foot of her reluctant kinsman and spat in his face.

The Levitical Law describes what should happen:

"Then the elders of his city shall call him, and speak unto him: and if he stand to it, and say, I like not to take her;

"Then shall his brother's wife come unto him in the presence of the elders, and loose his shoe from off his foot, and spit in his face, and shall answer and say, So shall it be done unto that man that will not build up his brother's house.

"And his name shall be called in Israel, The house of him that hath his shoe loosed" (Deuteronomy 25:8-10).

Though it is not recorded in the biblical account, Flavius Josephus wrote that Ruth took his shoe and spat in his face. In so doing, the way was cleared for Boaz to purchase the land and to purchase a wife:

"And Boaz said unto the elders, and unto all the people, Ye are witnesses this day, that I have bought all that was Elimelech's and all that was Chilion's and Mahlon's, of the hand of Naomi. Moreover Ruth the Moabitess, the wife of Mahlon, have I purchased to be my wife, to raise up the name of the dead upon his inheritance, that the name of the dead be not cut off from among his brethren, and from the gate of his place: ye are witnesses this day" (Ruth 4:9,10).

What a magnificent picture to be ultimately fulfilled by the great Kinsman Redeemer, the Lord Jesus Christ! Through His death at Calvary, He not only paved the way for the redemption of the land, but He provided the means whereby we might be redeemed as His Gentile bride.

It is difficult to say, from a prophetic perspective, who is represented by the other kinsman that turned down his right of first choice to be a kinsman redeemer. Let me suggest the possibility that the other kinsman remained unnamed and that his relationship remained unrevealed for a reason.

Since Ruth took his shoe and spat in his face, may I suggest the possibility that Lucifer, the mighty cherub who, according to the Scripture, was second only to God before his fall, might be the prophetic fulfillment of the unnamed relative. At least he comes nearer to the description as we see Ruth approach the kinsman, take his shoe, and spit in his face.

The symbol of the shoe represented one who lost his right of redemption. I guess we could say he was "de-feeted." Pardon me for saying so, but I can think of nothing that would give me greater pleasure than to be allowed to approach the defeated Satan, himself, and spit in his face. That is the prophecy to be found in the Mosaic covenant concerning the Kinsman Redeemer.

To the royal couple there was born a son. They called his name Obed, which means "servant or worker." From a prophetic perspective, he is typical of the eternal plan and purpose of God.

In the last chapter of the Bible, the Scripture describes God's plan for us:

"And there shall be no more curse: but the throne of God and of the Lamb shall be in it; and his servants shall serve him" (Revelation 22:3).

There it is. After this heaven and earth have passed away and the new heaven and earth are established, we shall live forever in the presence of God and we shall serve Him, thus fulfilling the prophetic meaning of the name Obed.

Finally, may I say, we owe a lot to the Jewish people. Gentile Christianity owes its existence to them. Let us be like Ruth. Let us be a loyal companion. Let us be a friend. For one day Israel will have her land and we will have our Kinsman Redeemer.

Chapter Nine

Barak and Deborah

During the four hundred years from Joshua to David, fourteen significant leaders, referred to as judges, were called upon to rescue Israel from oppression. They were Othniel, Ehud, Shamgar, Deborah, Barak, Gideon, Tola, Jair, Jephthah, Ibzan, Elon, Abdon, Samson, and Samuel. Each judge represented not only a time of deliverance for Israel but a prophetic scenario as well. Among these messiah figures, Barak and Deborah are especially significant. Barak was given special mention along with the other great men of faith in Hebrews 11:

"And what shall I more say? for the time would fail me to tell of Gideon, and of Barak, and of Samson, and of Jephthae; of David also, and Samuel, and of the prophets:

"Who through faith subdued kingdoms, wrought righteousness, obtained promises, stopped the mouths of lions,

"Quenched the violence of fire, escaped the edge of the sword, out of weakness were made strong, waxed valiant in fight, turned to flight the armies of the aliens.

"Women received their dead raised to life again: and others were tortured, not accepting deliverance; that they might obtain a better resurrection" (Hebrews 11:32-35).

These heroes were upheld as examples of a faith that transcends the works of the Law. They are shown as a great assembly — a cloud of witnesses — watching us as we live our lives for Christ. Since they are watching, we are urged to keep the faith — to be loyal and faithful to our Savior:

"Wherefore seeing we also are compassed about with so great a cloud of witnesses, let us lay aside every weight, and the sin which doth so easily beset us, and let us run with patience the race that is set before us,

"Looking unto Jesus the author and finisher of our faith; who for the joy that was set before him endured the cross, despising the shame, and is set down at the right hand of the throne of God" (Hebrews 12:1,2).

Barak's name is listed among those who watch and cheer us on. Though we find him not as brave as one would hope, it is made clear that the Lord looks beyond temporary human frailty and considers the underlying character that drives a man toward greatness. These lessons teach us that God does not keep us from difficulty, but rather allows them to provide us an opportunity to excel. May we be worthy of great faith in the face of trial.

Barak's Name

Barak's name means "lightning flashing." Perhaps this alludes to the coming of Christ in power and great glory. One is reminded of Matthew's description of Christ's return:

"For as the lightning cometh out of the east, and shineth even unto the west; so shall also the coming of the Son of man be" (Matthew 24:27).

With the underlying possibility that Barak represents a type of Christ, let us consider his story:

"And the children of Israel again did evil in the sight of the LORD, when Ehud was dead.

"And the LORD sold them into the hand of Jabin king of Canaan, that reigned in Hazor; the captain of whose host was Sisera, which dwelt in Harosheth of the Gentiles.

"And the children of Israel cried unto the LORD: for he had nine hundred chariots of iron; and twenty years he mightily oppressed the children of Israel" (Judges 4:1-3).

Over and over again throughout Israel's early history, there were times of unfaithfulness. Living in a land that flowed with milk and honey, the people would slide into idolatry, bring on the judgment of God, repent, and see revival — only to become prosperous and fall into idolatry again. Each time, God would raise up a deliverer — a messiah figure — to turn the attention of the people back to Himself and His promise of a future ultimate Savior.

On that occasion, God allowed Jabin, king of Canaan, to oppress the nation for twenty long years.

The length of this oppression shows the gravity of the situation. Israel needed to learn a hard lesson. More than that, however, Jabin's twenty-year reign of terror over Israel seems to prophetically correspond with the past twenty centuries, during which time Gentiles have oppressed the Jewish people.

Notice that since the Romans scattered the Jews among the nations, they have become more determined to serve the Lord. They have been cured of idolatry — so much so that they even rejected God's offer of a new covenant through Jesus Christ. They cling with tenacity to the Mosaic Law.

The Prophetess, Deborah

There was not a man willing to rally the nation against Jabin's oppression for twenty years. Not finding a man, God called a woman to initiate revival:

"And Deborah, a prophetess, the wife of Lapidoth, she judged Israel at that time.
"And she dwelt under the palm tree of Deborah between Ramah and Bethel in mount Ephraim: and the children of Israel came up to her for judgment" (Judges 4:4,5).

Deborah appears to be a prophetic type of Israel. Her name means "to arrange, in the sense of orderly motion." It means "to be a spokesman, to teach, to tell, to think, to work." These characteristics also speak of Israel — called of God to be the Chosen People; to rule as a benefit over all mankind; and to teach the human race about God. They were chosen to teach, to tell, to think, and to work for the good of all men.

Though not appreciated, the Jews have provided guidance for mankind down through history. They gave the human race civil law. They have advised kings from behind the scenes and taught nations the difference between right and wrong. They have provided the greatest guidebook of all — the Bible. Furthermore, many of the great inventions have been discovered and developed by Jews. Many great benefits to humanity in the areas of music, science, communications, transportation, high technology, medicine, and government resulted from the mental genius of the Jews. Yes, Deborah appears to be a prophetic picture of the nation of Israel.

She was the wife of Lapidoth which means "to shine." The term is also explained as a "burning lamp or flame, a torch, or lightning." Her husband's name is well suited to Barak which similarly means "lightning flashing." We are reminded that when Christ returns in power and great glory, His eyes will appear as flames of fire. The description is that of the *shekinah* glory — God's presence among Israel.

Deborah dwelt under a special palm tree between Ramah and Bethel (Judges 4:5). The word Ramah means "a high place" — a "seat of idolatry." On the other hand, Bethel means "the house of God." That is exactly where Israel has dwelt throughout history, between idolatry and serving the Lord. Also in that regard, Deborah appears to be a prophetic view of Israel.

As a woman of faith and prayer, she was divinely commissioned to summon Barak and inform him that God was going to deliver Jabin into his hand. After twenty years this appeared to be an impossibility. Jabin's army had 900 chariots of iron! However, this did not deter Deborah:

"And she sent and called Barak the son of Abinoam out of Kedeshnaphtali, and said unto him, Hath not the LORD God of Israel commanded, saying, Go and draw toward mount Tabor, and take with thee ten thousand men of the children of Naphtali and of the children of Zebulun?

"And I will draw unto thee to the river Kishon Sisera, the captain of Jabin's army, with his chariots and his multitude; and I will deliver him into thine hand.

"And Barak said unto her, If thou wilt go with me, then I will go: but if thou wilt not go with me, then I will not go.

"And she said, I will surely go with thee: notwithstanding the journey that thou takest shall not be for thine honor; for the LORD shall sell Sisera into the hand of a woman. And Deborah arose, and went with Barak to Kedesh.

"And Barak called Zebulun and Naphtali to Kedesh; and he went up with ten thousand men at his feet: and Deborah went up with him" (Judges 4:6-10).

Barak was willing to lead the battle under one condition — that Deborah would ride beside him. Some have suggested he wanted to "hide behind a woman's skirt" — a term for cowardice. Barak knew that Deborah could offer courage for an army ill equipped for waging a war against 900 chariots of iron. Nevertheless, Deborah accused him of having a measure of cowardice and predicted that Sisera, Jabin's captain, would fall at the hands of a woman. Barak would not get the glory for the victory. The glory would go to — not just another warrior, but a woman!

The prophetess commissioned Barak to lead the Israel's army against Sisera. The battle took place in the Valley of Megiddo, just west of Mount Tabor. From "Har Megiddo" (hill of Megiddo) comes the more familiar term, Armageddon. Therefore, this historic battle sets the precedent for that ultimate future war of the end-time. North of Mount Tabor lies a valley where Heber lived:

"Now Heber the Kenite, which was of the children of Hobab the father in law of Moses, had severed himself from the Kenites, and pitched his tent unto the plain of Zaanaim, which is by Kedesh.

"And they showed Sisera that Barak the son of Abinoam was gone up to mount Tabor.

"And Sisera gathered together all his chariots, even nine hundred chariots of iron, and all the people that were with him, from Harosheth of the Gentiles unto the river of Kishon" (Judges 4:11-13).

Barak and Deborah gathered 10,000 men on top of Mount Tabor, which lies near the east end of the Megiddo Valley. Sisera rallied his army, along with his 900 chariots of iron, near the Kishon River which runs beneath Mount Carmel near the west end of the valley:

"And Deborah said unto Barak, Up; for this is the day in which the LORD hath delivered Sisera into thine hand: is not

the LORD gone out before thee? So Barak went down from mount Tabor, and ten thousand men after him.

"And the LORD discomfited Sisera, and all his chariots, and all his host, with the edge of the sword before Barak; so that Sisera lighted down off his chariot, and fled away on his feet.

"But Barak pursued after the chariots, and after the host, unto Harosheth of the Gentiles: and all the host of Sisera fell upon the edge of the sword; and there was not a man left" (Judges 4:14-16).

As the battle began, Barak and his forces came down the mountain from the east. The scene appears to be apocalyptic. It reminds us that one day our Savior will come down from the east with the armies of heaven. Barak appears to be a prophetic picture of Christ, who will come one day to fight the final battle in the valley of Armageddon.

The Hail Storm

Here is another exciting part of the story. When the battle between Barak and Sisera was engaged, a terrific storm of lightning, rain, high winds and hail was unleashed against Sisera and his army. They had to advance into the storm while Barak's men had their backs to the deluge.

Flavius Josephus wrote about it 2,000 years ago in his book, *The Antiquities of the Jews*: "So the battle began, and when they were come to a close fight, there came down from heaven a great storm with a vast quantity of rain and hail. And the wind blew the rain in the face of the Canaanites, and so darkened their eyes that their arrows and slings were of no advantage to them, nor would the coldness of the air permit the soldiers to make use of their swords ..."

At the same time, Josephus said that the storm offered no problem for the Israelites "... because it came in their backs." Here is another portrayal of the future Battle of Armageddon as vials of God's wrath are poured out upon an unbelieving world. The armies of Armageddon will face the most devastating thunderstorm in history:

"And there were voices, and thunders, and lightnings; and there was a great earthquake, such as was not since men were upon the earth, so mighty an earthquake, and so great.

"And every island fled away, and the mountains were not found.

"And there fell upon men a great hail out of heaven, every stone about the weight of a talent: and men blasphemed God because of the plague of the hail; for the plague thereof was exceeding great" (Revelation 16:18, 20, 21).

In the predicted Battle of Armageddon, chunks of ice weighing up to a hundred pounds will fall upon the enemy.

According to the account given by Flavius Josephus, Barak's soldiers took courage as they realized that God had come to their aid. The swollen Kishon River flooded the area creating a vast, muddy field. The 900 chariots of iron, manned by the Gentiles, bogged down in the mire. In the concluding hours of the battle, the Gentile oppressors died at the hands of the Israelites.

Sisera Escapes — Almost

While Barak and his soldiers slaughtered the oppressors, Sisera left his entrapped chariot and fled on foot. Running along the valley north of Mt. Tabor, he came to the tent of Jael, the wife of Heber, the Kenite:

"Howbeit Sisera fled away on the feet to the tent of Jael the wife of Heber the Kenite: for there was peace between Jabin the king of Hazor and the house of Heber the Kenite.

"And Jael went out to meet Sisera, and said unto him, Turn in, my lord, turn in to me; fear not. And when he had turned in unto her into the tent, she covered him with a mantle.

"And he said unto her, Give me, I pray thee, a little water to drink; for I am thirsty. And she opened a bottle of milk, and gave him drink, and covered him.

"Again he said unto her, Stand in the door of the tent, and it shall be, when any man doth come and inquire of thee, and say, Is there any man here? that thou shalt say, No" (Judges 4:17-20).

Jael Nails Him in the Temple

Sisera was tired and thirsty and felt secure in the hands of Jael. Little did he know that she planned his execution. The tired and weary Sisera laid down to rest and asked the woman to stand in the door of the tent to watch while he slept:

"Then Jael Heber's wife took a nail of the tent, and took an hammer in her hand, and went softly unto him, and smote the nail into his temples, and fastened it into the ground: for he was fast asleep and weary. So he died.

"And, behold, as Barak pursued Sisera, Jael came out to meet him, and said unto him, Come, and I will show thee the

man whom thou seekest. And when he came into her tent, behold, Sisera lay dead, and the nail was in his temples" (Judges 4:21,22).

As he drifted off to sleep, Jael took a hammer and a large iron nail (a tent stake) and drove it through his temple. She nailed him to the ground. She put a mark on his forehead which resulted in his death. One cannot say that it represents the mark of the beast, but it certainly seems to fit the story!

By the way, the wicked Sisera was nailed in the temple — the temple of his head, that is. It may be a prophetic picture of where the Antichrist will be when Christ returns — in the Jewish temple. Religious Jews wear a small wooden box on their foreheads as a reminder of the Ark of the Covenant which once rested in the Temple. Maybe that is why the forehead is called a temple!

So, Sisera was nailed in the temple. The entire event smacks of Armageddon when the armies of heaven come like lightning to establish the Kingdom of Christ on earth.

Jael was a Kenite. She was not a Jew. She was a Gentile of the children of Jethro, the father-in-law of Moses. She was related to the Gentile bride of Moses. The name Jael means "to ascend." Her husband's name, Heber, means "society or community." She appears to represent New Testament Christianity, the Gentile bride who (as a society or community of believers) will ascend and return one day with Christ at the Battle of Armageddon.

Could this be a prophecy of the defeat of the Antichrist at the hands of Gentile Christianity? Though Barak won the battle against the army of Gentiles, their leader, Sisera, escaped — only to be nailed by Jael. Perhaps Sisera is a type of the Antichrist.

A Woman Killed Abimelech

The story about the defeat of Sisera at the hands of a woman coincides with other Antichrist figures who faced defeat at the hands of women. First was Abimelech, one of Gideon's seventy sons. After Gideon's death, Abimelech aspired to the throne which had been declined by his illustrious father. He approached the elders of Shechem and applied for the job. Having respect for Gideon, the elders approved and made Abimelech their king. His first order of business was to murder his brothers — all sixty-nine of them. However, one escaped — Jotham. It is an amazing story, filled with prophetic overtones. However, the most bizarre part of the scriptural account is that Abimelech was killed by a woman:

"And Abimelech came unto the tower, and fought against it, and went hard unto the door of the tower to burn it with fire.

"And a certain woman cast a piece of a millstone upon Abimelech's head, and all to brake his skull.

"Then he called hastily unto the young man his armourbearer, and said unto him, Draw thy sword, and slay me, that men say not of me, A woman slew him. And his young man thrust him through, and he died" (Judges 9:52-54).

Again, it was a woman who killed another prophetic type of the Antichrist by striking him in the head. Yes, the great battle of Barak in the Valley of Megiddo presents an excellent prophetic scenario of that future battle — the awesome Armageddon.

Chapter Ten

Jotham and The Crown of Thorns

By nine o'clock in the morning, our Lord had been arrested and tried before the Sanhedrin, Herod and Pilate. All were "kangaroo courts." No substantial charges could be made. No credible witnesses or evidence could be presented. Yet, He was condemned.

Hardened soldiers stripped Him of His outer garment, and laid the Roman scourge across His backside with a vengeance. Jesus was flogged, dressed in a makeshift royal robe, given a stick for a scepter and crowned with a wreath of thorns. He was led out before Pilate and an angry crowd who were drunk with a blood-thirst:

"Pilate therefore went forth again, and saith unto them, Behold, I bring him forth to you, that ye may know that I find no fault in him.

"Then came Jesus forth, wearing the crown of thorns, and the purple robe. And Pilate saith unto them, Behold the man!" (John 19:4,5).

Every Easter we are reminded of the arrest, trial and crucifixion of our Lord. We imagine the scene — the purple robe and crown of thorns and realize that Christ was mocked as the King of the Jews. We know that He really is their King, but have we understood the significance of the thorns?

Adam's Fall

In order to fully comprehend God's plan for Israel's King to wear a crown made out of thorns, we must follow the trail back into the pages of the Old Testament. There we find the thorns associated with the Antichrist — a result of the fall of Adam. Until the fall, the earth did not produce thorns:

"And unto Adam he said, Because thou hast hearkened unto the voice of thy wife, and hast eaten of the tree, of which I commanded thee, saying, Thou shalt not eat of it: cursed is the ground for thy sake; in sorrow shalt thou eat of it all the days of thy life;

"Thorns also and thistles shall it bring forth to thee; and thou shalt eat the herb of the field" (Genesis 3:17,18).

From this point in Scripture, thorns and thistles appear to be associated with both the curse and the seed of the serpent — the Antichrist.

Isaac's Substitute Ram

The next time the thorn bush appears in the Bible, Abraham is about to slay his son. An angel stops him and points out a substitute sacrifice. Abraham saw a ram caught in a thicket. Think of it! The substitute sacrifice was caught in a thorny bush.

The Burning Bush

Then, there is the thorn bush on Sinai that burned, but was not consumed. According to the late M. R. De Haan, it was prophetic of Israel who has gone through the fire without being consumed.

The Ark and Tabernacle

The bramble or thorn bush is a member of the acacia wood family. It was the type of wood used in building both the Ark of the Covenant and the Tabernacle and is typical of our humanity. At our very best, the human race is nothing better than a bramble bush. Oh, how unworthy we are! We are just producers of thorns and thistles.

Thorns and the Enemy

In the books of Numbers and Joshua, thorns are used to describe an enemy — *"... thorns in your sides"* and *"... thorns in your eyes:"*

"But if ye will not drive out the inhabitants of the land from before you; then it shall come to pass, that those which ye let remain of them shall be pricks in your eyes, and thorns in your sides, and shall vex you in the land wherein ye dwell" (Numbers 33:55).

"Know for a certainty that the LORD your God will no more drive out any of these nations from before you; but they shall be snares and traps unto you, and scourges in your sides, and thorns in your eyes, until ye perish from off this good land which the LORD your God hath given you" (Joshua 23:13).

Thorns and Fire

In both Exodus and the Psalms, thorns became associated with a judgment of fire — a reminder of hell:

"If fire break out, and catch in thorns, so that the stacks of corn, or the standing corn, or the field, be consumed therewith; he that kindled the fire shall surely make restitution" (Exodus 22:6).

"They compassed me about like bees; they are quenched as the fire of thorns: for in the name of the LORD I will destroy them" (Psalm 118:12).

Here, we note that thorns are a part of God's judgment upon a wicked and sinful humanity.

Thorns and Snares

In the book of Proverbs, thorns are associated with traps and snares:

"The way of the slothful man is as an hedge of thorns: but the way of the righteous is made plain" (Proverbs 15:19).

"Thorns and snares are in the way of the froward: he that doth keep his soul shall be far from them" (Proverbs 22:5).

Thorns in the Day of Judgment

As we progress through the Scriptures, the use of thorns becomes even clearer. Isaiah uses the symbolic "thorn" eleven times. Most of the passages have to do with scattering the Jews among the nations. Also, a promise is given that the Messiah — the Holy One — will come someday and destroy the evil one and his thorns:

"And the light of Israel shall be for a fire, and his Holy One for a flame: and it shall burn and devour his thorns and his briers in one day;

"And shall consume the glory of his forest, and of his fruitful field, both soul and body: and they shall be as when a standardbearer fainteth.

"And the rest of the trees of his forest shall be few, that a child may write them.

"And it shall come to pass in that day, that the remnant of Israel, and such as are escaped of the house of Jacob, shall no more again stay upon him that smote them; but shall stay upon the LORD, the Holy One of Israel, in truth" (Isaiah 10:17-20).

Isaiah promises that in the future Messianic Kingdom, thorns will have no place:

"Instead of the thorn shall come up the fir tree, and instead of the brier shall come up the myrtle tree: and it shall be to the LORD for a name, for an everlasting sign that shall not be cut off" (Isaiah 55:13).

Thorns and Society

Micah describes world conditions following the Rapture of the Church. Israel is left behind and finds herself in the midst of a Luciferian society with no friends. Here, Micah associates the thorn with the wicked and their leader — the future Antichrist:

"The good man is perished out of the earth: and there is none upright among men: they all lie in wait for blood; they hunt every man his brother with a net.

"That they may do evil with both hands earnestly, the prince asketh, and the judge asketh for a reward; and the great man, he uttereth his mischievous desire: so they wrap it up.

"The best of them is as a brier: the most upright is sharper

than a thorn hedge: the day of thy watchmen and thy visitation cometh; now shall be their perplexity" (Micah 7:2-4).

The brier and thorn hedge are used to describe the wickedness of society after all the saints have been removed.

The Hebrew term for *"perished"* (v.2) is *avad* [אבד] meaning "to disappear." The world may think the saints are among those who have perished when, in fact, they have been removed from the earth. In verse four, a reference is made to the prophesied invasion from the north — the Battle of Gog and Magog. Micah writes, *"... the day of thy watchmen and thy visitation cometh"* (v.4). The Hebrew term for *"watchmen"* is *mitzapeach* [מצפך], from which *tzaphon* [צפן] meaning "north," can be derived, leading some to suggest that the invasion could come from the north. Perhaps the Rapture will occur on the day of a great worldwide war which explodes in Northern Israel. Such a conflagration could quickly spread around the world if nuclear weapons are used.

The Sons of Gideon

Thorns are also associated with the story of Gideon and his sons. It is perhaps the most vivid account of thorns in Scripture used to describe the reign of the Antichrist. The story begins about a hundred years before the saga of Saul and David.

The northern tribes offered a crown to Gideon. The book of Judges records the victory of Gideon's three hundred soldiers over the hordes of Midianites with what can only be described as a miraculous military strategy.

At first Gideon had over 32,000 men under his command, but God asked him to eliminate the unnecessary troops. After only two sessions, in which those who wanted to leave and those who were ill-prepared were sent home. Gideon was left with only three hundred soldiers. Each was armed with a clay pitcher, a light and a horn, yet Gideon managed to rout out the enemy. The startled and frightened Midianites killed many of their own men in the stampede to escape the lights and sounds.

When Gideon was first chosen to deliver Israel from the Midianites, he could hardly believe it. He was not the type that one would normally choose to be a leader, yet the Lord called him a *"... mighty man of valor"* (Judges 6:12). He was so shocked by the Lord's assessment of his character and so stunned by his calling, that he had to put out a fleece just to make sure he was not mistaken. As the story goes, Gideon was asked to be their king. Though he was grateful for their appreciation, he kindly declined the throne, saying that the Lord should be the only King in Israel.

The Wicked Abimelech

After Gideon's death, the evil Abimelech, one of Gideon's seventy sons, approached the elders and asked that he be given the kingship once offered to his father. As an honor to Gideon, Abimelech was installed as their king.

His reign, however, was a complete disaster. He ruled for a little over three years and brought misery to the nation. Abimelech's sordid story appears to be a prophetic preview of the Antichrist.

Shortly after his coronation, this wicked son of Gideon ordered a band of men to seek out and execute his brothers in order to keep them from becoming a political threat. However, Gideon's youngest son, Jotham, was able to escape.

According to the biblical account, Jotham went to Shechem and spoke to the elders of Israel. They ruled the nation from atop Mount Gerizim, overlooking the city of Shechem. It was the place where Joshua read the Law to the people and where, in later years, a Samaritan temple was built. It rivaled the temple at Jerusalem. Gerizim represented a substitute capital for the nation of Israel — a prophetic pattern for the throne of the Antichrist.

Jotham, youngest son of Gideon and half-brother to the wicked Abimelech, climbed to the top of Mount Gerizim and declared a parable before the elders of Israel. His parable against Abimelech offers a magnificent, prophetic overview of Israel's quest for a messiah. They were so anxious for the Messiah to come they chose the wrong man.

Abimelech, of course, did not last long. His three-year reign is typical of the future Antichrist. According to the prophets, from the abomination of desolation to the conclusion of Antichrist's reign will be about three and one-half years.

The story concludes with a tale about Abimelech's death. One day, in the midst of a battle, a woman dropped a rock from a window near the top of a tower and hit Abimelech on the head. In his dying moments he turned to one of his soldiers and asked him to take his life, lest others learned that he died at the hands of a woman:

"Draw thy sword, and slay me, that men say not of me, A woman slew him. And his young man thrust him through, and he died" (Judges 9:54).

His soldier obliged, thus ending the life of the wicked King Abimelech. So wicked was his reign that he was not even listed among the kings of Israel.

Jotham's Parable of the Thorn

Jotham begins his story to the elders of Israel with a parable. He likens the people of Israel to a forest of trees. Five trees are mentioned here and each one of them is typical of Israel — the olive tree, fig tree, grape vine, bramble bush, and cedars of Lebanon. Each tree, in its own way, seems to reveal certain characteristics about the nation. The bramble, a thorny bush, is used to describe the great betrayer — the Antichrist. In this story, that position is reserved for Abimelech. Jotham begins:

"The trees went forth on a time to anoint a king over them; and they said unto the olive tree, Reign thou over us.
"But the olive tree said unto them, Should I leave my fat-

ness, wherewith by me they honor God and man, and go to be promoted over the trees?

"And the trees said to the fig tree, Come thou, and reign over us.

"But the fig tree said unto them, Should I forsake my sweetness, and my good fruit, and go to be promoted over the trees?

"Then said the trees unto the vine, Come thou, and reign over us.

"And the vine said unto them, Should I leave my wine, which cheereth God and man, and go to be promoted over the trees?

"Then said all the trees unto the bramble, Come thou, and reign over us.

"And the bramble said unto the trees, If in truth ye anoint me king over you, then come and put your trust in my shadow; and if not, let fire come out the bramble, and devour the cedars of Lebanon" (Judges 9:8-15).

When the olive tree was asked to be king over all the forest, it refused by saying that it was more important to use its oil for the glory of God. Olive oil was used to fuel the seven lamps of the golden lampstand in the Tabernacle. That light was typical of the *shekinah* glory of God.

When the grape vine was asked to be king over the forest, it declined by saying that the fruit it bore brought happiness to both God and man. Prophetically, it is the blood of Jesus Christ — the prophetic fulfillment of the grape that has brought happiness to both God and man. Christ became the atonement for our sins.

The bramble bush, a member of the acacia tree family, was asked to be king over all the forest. Unfortunately, it agreed, saying to all the other trees of the forest, *"If in truth ye anoint me king over you, then come and put your trust in my shadow"* (Judges 9:15). Thus, the most lowly and despised of all the trees, wanted to drag the rest of the forest down to its low estate. That was the only way it could be exalted above the others. Prophetically, that is what the Antichrist will do.

These five trees, representing the nation of Israel, are used over and over throughout the Bible. They offer more than a mere explanation that the elders made a wrong choice. They actually demonstrate the character and reign of the Antichrist.

Please note that in his parable, Jotham begins with an invitation to the best tree and ends the parable with an invitation to the worst. How typical, of not only the nation of Israel, but also of the human race. Over the centuries man has become progressively worse — proving to be a failure in every generation. The history of humankind has been filled with a continual degeneration. This is true, especially of God's Chosen People. They have proven themselves (as have we all) unworthy of leadership in God's creation:

"All we like sheep have gone astray; we have turned every one to his own way; and the LORD hath laid on Him the iniquity of us all" (Isaiah 53:6).

The Olive Tree

Among all of the forest, the olive tree stands for peace. Its branch, representing the Jews, has been a symbol of peace among nations down through the centuries. After the great Flood, Noah sent a dove in search of life and it brought back a leaf of an olive tree. This was God's way of saying to Noah that His judgment was past and that a new world filled with peace awaited him.

The olive is not a pretty tree. Its branches are gnarled and twisted. However, it will grow where no other trees will. It is enduring and persevering. Where other trees would have given up and died long ago, the olive tree clings to life and hope. Today, on the Mount of Olives, there are olive trees still growing, still alive, which are said to be over 2,000 years old. One tree in the Garden of Gethsemane is four feet in diameter. It is estimated to be 3,000 years old — still alive and still bearing fruit. Though its branches are gnarled and twisted and though much of the heart of the tree has rotted away, its hollow trunk still clings to life. What a prophetic picture of the nation of Israel — still clinging to life and hope after 3,000 years of suffering! Though the Israeli nation does not seem to be a thing of beauty among the nations of the world, she still clings to life, in the hope that her fruit will one day declare the glory of God.

According to the *World Book Encyclopedia*, when the olive tree is harvested, its branches are shaken or beaten. This seems to be a prophetic portrayal of Israel, who must yield its fruit through suffering. Also, the olive's oil can only give its light when burned.

Only one flower in every 100 will bear fruit. Most of the flowers on the olive tree will be imperfect and will fall off — rejected. In fact, Job makes a reference to this phenomenon: *"He shall ... cast off his flower as the olive"* (Job 15:33).

Just think — only one flower in every 100 bears fruit. Furthermore, it is said that fruit is made better by grafting a cultivated olive branch into the stalk of a wild seedling. The Apostle Paul made a similar reference in Romans chapter 11, when he referred to the nation of Israel as an olive tree.

In that chapter, he turned the process around. He wrote that a wild olive branch (Gentile Christianity) had been grafted into the good olive tree. Historically, it is true that we have our roots in Judaism. Paul was teaching that God cast Israel aside only temporarily. He plans to graft them back into that tree again someday. God is not finished with Israel. At Christ's Second Coming, the tree will be made whole again.

The Fig Tree

The fig tree was among the first trees mentioned in the Bible. Its leaves were used as a covering for the sinful Adam and Eve. When the glory was gone, they sewed fig leaves together to make clothes. The olive tree was typical of God's glory, and the fig tree was symbolic of the substitute covering wrought by the hands of man. As a fig tree, Israel was a substitute human race chosen by God to provide a covering for the sins of men. The Hebrew word for covering is also translated "atonement," making Christ our atonement for sin.

Unlike the other trees, the flower of the fig tree is located in the fruit. In fact, the fruit appears first and then the flower. Prophetically, it represents the con-

cept that the real beauty of the believer can be found
in the fruit he bears. Do you want to be pleasing to
God? Then be a soul winner. The only flowers which
are pleasing to God are those which are found in the
fruit. Unfortunately, as a fig tree, Israel bore no fruit.
The nation did not take the message of God's love
and grace to the Gentiles.

As a prophetic picture of this, Jesus told the parable of a fig tree. The story is found in Luke 13:6-9.
He said that a man who owned a vineyard planted a
fig tree in the midst of it and had his gardener to care
for it. The first year, he found that it bore no fruit.
The second year it bore no fruit. In the third year, it
again proved fruitless. Finally, the owner of the vineyard then said to his gardener, *"Cut it down. Why
cumbereth it the ground?"* This is exactly what God
has done with the Jewish people. Because they bore
no fruit, God had the nation of Israel cut down and
scattered among the nations of the world for the past
2,000 years.

According to the *Zondervan Pictorial Encyclopedia of the Bible*, the fig tree produces two crops each
year. The winter figs ripen in May and June, and the
summer figs are harvested in the months of August
and September. Two crops! Perhaps they are typical
of the First and Second Advents of Christ. When He
came the first time Israel had borne no fruit. However, when He comes the second time, they will.

When the fig tree was asked to be king over the
forest, it refused, stating that it was more important

to bear fruit than it was to be king. This should have been typical of Israel — busy bearing fruit for the kingdom of God. However, when Jesus came to inspect the fig tree, He noted that it had borne no fruit:

"And when he saw a fig tree in the way, he came to it, and found nothing thereon, but leaves only, and said unto it, Let no fruit grow on thee henceforward for ever. And presently the fig tree withered away" (Matthew 21:19).

He found nothing but leaves. As a result, Christ placed a curse upon the fig tree. The prophecy here is that Israel was to be plucked from her land and scattered among the nations. Fortunately, Christ used that fig tree again in the Matthew 24 to represent the return of the Chosen People to their Promised Land.

"Now learn a parable of the fig tree; When his branch is yet tender, and putteth forth leaves, ye know that summer is nigh:

"So likewise ye, when ye shall see all these things, know that it is near, even at the doors.

"Verily I say unto you, This generation shall not pass, till all these things be fulfilled" (Matthew 24:32-34).

He noted that one day, the fig will revive and bear fruit. In effect, Jesus was saying that when the nation of Israel comes back to life again and the Jews return to their land, then you know that the fulfillment of all Bible prophecy is about to come to pass. When these things happen, that generation will see the return of Christ. Many feel we have been living in that generation since 1948. What a message! — this prophecy of the fig tree.

The Grape Vine

The third tree in Jotham's parable is a grape vine. Though it was not as tall and stately as the trees before it, nevertheless, its fruit brought refreshment and delight to both God and man. The prophetic fulfillment can be seen in the life of Jesus Christ who said:

"I am the vine, ye are the branches" (John 15:5).

The fruit of the olive is burned to declare the glory of God. The fruit of the fig represents a covering for the souls of men. The fruit of the vine is a prophetic picture of the blood of Christ, which was shed for our sins and has indeed become pleasing to God and man. It is through His blood that we are given eternal life.

The crucifixion satisfied the mandate that sin should bring forth death. It allows us the opportunity to sidestep the verdict and live forever. Christ paid the ultimate price for us. He was our stand-in at the judgment. If we accept Him as our Savior, He can save us from eternal death and give us eternal life! The estrangement between God and man was dissolved at Calvary. Indeed, Christ has brought happiness to both God and man. Instead of a throne, Christ chose the cross. As the grape, Christ allowed Himself to be crushed for our benefit. What appears to be defeat, actually becomes a victory.

The Bramble Bush

That brings us to the fourth tree in Jotham's parable — the bramble bush. There is no fruit to the bramble bush — only thorns. It is typical of the nation of Israel who will one day (in its unbelief) produce the Antichrist.

The prophecy takes us to Calvary. The bramble bush is made into a crown of thorns and sits upon the head of Jesus Christ. In Jotham's parable, the bramble was asked to become king over all the trees in the forest. Well, at Calvary that bramble bush was made into a crown to be worn by the King. Look at it! See it in your imagination as it presses down upon the brow of the matchless Son of God. See it sit there in all of its shame, piercing the flesh, bringing the blood. It was not a crown made out of olive wood; it was a crown made from a bramble bush. It was not a crown made of fig wood; it was made from a bramble bush. It was not a crown made out of grape vine; it was a lowly bramble bush!

In Jotham's parable, when the bramble was invited to be their king, it replied, *"If in truth ye anoint me king over you, then come and put your trust in my shadow ..."* (Judges 9:15). In prophetic fulfillment, see the Savior hanging there in humility beneath the shadow of the bramble bush. Watch, as it is exalted upon His head. Watch, as it draws His blood. Hear His pitiful cry, *"My God, my God, why hast thou forsaken me?"* It looked as if the bramble bush was triumphant and that the olive tree, the fig tree, and the vine will be forever defeated. It looks as if that *"Root of David,"* that *"Rod out of the stem of Jesse,"* that great *"Branch"* was to be forever humiliated by that crown of a bramble bush. How sad! When the bramble bush answered the request of the other trees, it said, *"... put your trust in my shadow: and if not, let fire come out of the bramble, and devour the cedars of Lebanon."* It did not say, "I will devour the olive tree." It did not say that it would burn the fig tree, or the vine. It said, *"I will devour the cedars of Lebanon."*

Forty years later, a fire devoured the great cedars of Lebanon, just like the parable said it would. The fulfillment of that prophecy came when the Romans burned the Temple to the ground. The doors of the Temple were made out of cedar wood from Lebanon.

The prophet Zechariah also predicted it:

"Open wide thy doors, O Lebanon, that the fire may devour thy cedars" (Zechariah 11:1).

One day, yet in the future, that bramble bush will be made king. As the wicked Abimelech ruled over Israel for some three years, the Antichrist will usurp the throne of God and will make himself to be ruler over Israel and the world.

That, however, is not the end of the story. Abimelech came to an inglorious end and so will that crown of thorns! When the rule of the Antichrist has run its course, the Savior who hung in shame upon that cross will return in power and great glory. Upon His head will sit — not a rugged crown of bramble bush, but a royal diadem:

"And I saw heaven opened, and behold a white horse; and he that sat upon him was called Faithful and True, and in righteousness he doth judge and make war.

"His eyes were as a flame of fire, and on his head were many crowns; and he had a name written, that no man knew, but he himself.

"And he was clothed with a vesture dipped in blood: and his name is called The Word of God.

"And the armies which were in heaven followed him upon white horses, clothed in fine linen, white and clean.

"And out of his mouth goeth a sharp sword, that with it he should smite the nations: and he shall rule them with a rod of iron: and he treadeth the winepress of the fierceness and wrath of Almighty God.

"And he hath on his vesture and on his thigh a name written, KING OF KINGS, AND LORD OF LORDS" (Rev. 19:11-16).

The bramble bush shall not be king! When the Lord of glory comes back to this earth, the olive tree will be exalted to proclaim the glory of God; the fig tree will be exalted to bear fruit; and the vine will be exalted to cheer God and man. In that day, Jesus Christ will be proclaimed King of kings, and Lord of lords! The bramble bush shall not be king! That is the prophecy behind the crown of thorns.

Chapter Eleven

Jephthah's Promise

Jephthah was listed as the ninth judge of Israel — a man rejected by his brothers only to return one day to become the head of their tribe. He is mentioned in Hebrews 11:32 among the great heroes of the faith:

"And what shall I more say? for the time would fail me to tell of Gideon, and of Barak, and of Samson, and of Jephthae ..."

Though Jephthah was the son of Gilead, his mother was not a legitimate member of the family. As a matter of fact, she was a harlot. When Gilead's legitimate sons grew up, they threw Jephthah out of their father's house and drove him from the city. He was a man rejected:

"Now Jephthah the Gileadite was a mighty man of valor, and he was the son of an harlot: and Gilead begat Jephthah.

"And Gilead's wife bare him sons; and his wife's sons grew up, and they thrust out Jephthah, and said unto him, Thou

shalt not inherit in our father's house; for thou art the son of a strange woman" (Judges 11:1,2).

In a similar way, Jesus Christ was rejected by the Jewish people. Though He was the virgin-born Son of God, He was accused of being an illegitimate son. In this regard, Jephthah appears to be a prophetic preview of Jesus Christ. Let us follow the story:

"And it was so, that when the children of Ammon made war against Israel, the elders of Gilead went to fetch Jephthah out of the land of Tob" (Judges 11:5).

In this verse, the rejected Jephthah was sought out when the big battle came. This verse tells us that they found him residing in the land of Tob. According to *Strong's Concordance* the word *"Tob"* means: "beautiful, best, better, bountiful, cheerful, at ease, fair, favor, fine, glad, good, graciously, joyful, kindness, loving, merry, most pleasant, precious, prosperity, sweet, wealth, welfare, and well favored!" What a magnificent picture of heaven! That is where Christ (the greater Jephthah) is residing today, after being rejected by His brethren, the Jews:

"And they said unto Jephthah, Come, and be our captain, that we may fight with the children of Ammon.

"And Jephthah said unto the elders of Gilead, Did not ye hate me, and expel me out of my father's house? and why are ye come unto me now when ye are in distress?

"And the elders of Gilead said unto Jephthah, Therefore we turn again to thee now, that thou mayest go with us, and fight against the children of Ammon, and be our head over all the inhabitants of Gilead." (Judges 11:6-8).

In these verses, the rejected Jephthah was promised that he could be their ruler. One day, the rejected Jesus will return in the midst of another big battle. When He comes that second time, He too will be accepted. He will be sought out by the Jewish people to become their ruler.

The name Jephthah means "to set free." Again, this is indicative of Christ, who came the first time 2,000 years ago to set us free from the bondage of sin. He will return one day to establish His kingdom upon the earth.

There is another part of the story which may also have prophetic significance. Jephthah vowed that if he were successful, he would offer a sacrifice to the Lord upon his return home:

"And Jephthah vowed a vow unto the Lord, and said, If thou shalt without fail deliver the children of Ammon into mine hands,"

"Then it shall be, that whatsoever cometh forth of the doors of my house to meet me, when I return in peace from the children of Ammon, shall surely be the LORD'S, and I will offer it up for a burnt offering" (Judges 11:30,31).

Perhaps he expected some animal around the house — a favorite lamb or calf. Jephthah won the war that day and upon his return home his daughter came out to meet him. She was his only child, and though he deeply regretted making the vow, he felt that he could not go back on his word. However, at this point may we be reminded of the Mosaic Law against the sacrifice of a human being:

"There shall not be found among you any one that maketh his son or his daughter to pass through the fire ..." (Deuteronomy 18:10).

We are not told that he specifically sacrificed his daughter. We are told only that he kept his vow:

"And it came to pass at the end of two months, that she returned unto her father, who did with her according to his vow which he had vowed: and she knew no man" (Judges 11:39).

It is the opinion of some scholars that Jephthah did not kill her, but that he dedicated her life to being a virgin. The verse says simply, *"she knew no man...."* She was never allowed to marry and produce children. In effect, he sacrificed any future children who might carry on the family name.

This appears to be prophetic of the bride of Christ after the battle of Armageddon. Perhaps that is why Jesus said there would be no marriage in heaven. In our new immortal bodies, we will not be given the ability of procreation:

"Jesus answered and said unto them, Ye do err, not knowing the scriptures, nor the power of God.
"For in the resurrection they neither marry, nor are given in marriage, but are as the angels of God in heaven" (Matthew 22:29,30).

Through faith in Christ, we may obtain eternal life. We will enjoy the adventures of eternity with our Savior. However, we will not be given the ability to bring forth children. The daughter of Jephthah appears to be prophetic of the future bride of Christ.

So, there you have it. Jephthah was rejected by his brethren, only to be sought after and accepted when the big battle came. Surely he is a type of Jesus Christ, who was once rejected by His brethren, and who will be accepted one day when He returns in power and great glory to win the battle of Armageddon.

Chapter Twelve

The Saga of Samson

Samson provides one of the strangest stories in the Old Testament. Though he was divinely appointed, his life would have come to an inglorious end had it not been for one last big push. On that fateful day, he killed 3,000 Philistines and lost his own life.

Some Jewish scholars have considered the story of Samson to be fictitious. A rabbi recently suggested that the four chapters of Samson's story were inserted into the book of Judges at a later date.

However bizarre the story of Samson seems to be, one need not question its authenticity. Even the New Testament, written in the first century, confirms its inclusion in the Bible. Some rabbis may not want to claim kin to Samson, but he is listed in the eleventh chapter of Hebrews as one of their heroes of the faith:

*"And what shall I more say? for the time would fail me to tell of Gideon, and of Barak, and of **Samson**, and of Jephthae; of David also, and Samuel, and of the prophets:*
"Who through faith subdued kingdoms, wrought righteousness, obtained promises, stopped the mouths of lions,
"Quenched the violence of fire, escaped the edge of the sword, out of weakness were made strong, waxed valiant in fight, turned to flight the armies of the aliens" (Hebrews 11:32-34).

In most respects, Samson typifies Israel. His reckless abandon for self-preservation has become a motto of their modern military.

The Samson Complex

Since 1948, the Israeli Defense Forces (IDF) have fought several major wars against Arab nations. During those conflicts, the rallying cry was centered around Masada where, in A.D. 73, some 960 Jews committed suicide rather than become slaves of the Romans. Taking up that theme, Israel's motto was "Masada shall never fall again." This attitude was referred to as the "Masada complex." However, since the 1973 Yom Kippur War, Israel has taken on a new and daring attitude — the "Samson complex." In their "Masada complex" the Israeli army vowed to die before they would submit to defeat. Now, however, the IDF vows that if they must die, they, like Samson, will take as many of their enemies with them as they can.

This new and dangerous attitude not only has a sense of suicide about it, as does the "Masada complex," but also exhibits an air of recklessness. One could sense the "Samson complex" at work when Israel bombed Baghdad's nuclear power plant in June

1981. Such an attitude also led Israel to annex the Golan Heights. Since then, Syria has refused to negotiate over the disputed territory. Many are convinced the stalemate will lead to war. Recognizing Israel's reckless attitude, let us consider the story of Samson and study the events surrounding his life.

Samson Is a Prophecy

Samson offers more than just a story. The life of Samson constitutes a prophetic example — typical of Israel who was chosen to produce the Messianic Era. Just as Samson was called of God to be a super man, Israel was called upon to be a super race.

The name Samson שמשון *Shemeshon* comes from the ancient root word שמש *Shemesh* (sun). He was born only a few miles from the village of Beth-Shemesh (house of the sun). His name is thought to mean, "like the sun," or "child of the sun." Perhaps David was alluding to Samson as he wrote that the rising sun *"... rejoiceth as a strong man to run a race"* (Psalm 19:5).

Samson's mother was barren. She was the fourth barren woman of seven listed in the Bible. These barren women of the Bible were Sarah, Rebekah, Rachel, Samson's unnamed mother, Hannah, Elizabeth and Mary. Together, they form a *menorah* design. Being the fourth, it appears that Samson's mother was chosen to produce the son who would fulfill the prophetic position of the servant lamp.

In our book, *The Mystery of the Menorah*, we noted

that this servant lamp held a special position on the seven-branched lampstand. Being the middle lamp, it was elevated above the others and designated as the *ner Elohim* — the lamp of God. Evidently, Samson was chosen to be a servant lamp.

The story of Samson, Israel's thirteenth judge, opens in the thirteenth chapter of the book of Judges:

"And there was a certain man of Zorah, of the family of the Danites, whose name was Manoah; and his wife was barren, and bare not.

"And the angel of the LORD appeared unto the woman, and said unto her, Behold now, thou art barren, and bearest not: but thou shalt conceive, and bear a son.

"Now therefore beware, I pray thee, and drink not wine nor strong drink, and eat not any unclean thing:

"For, lo, thou shalt conceive, and bear a son; and no razor shall come on his head: for the child shall be a Nazarite unto God from the womb: and he shall begin to deliver Israel out of the hand of the Philistines" (Judges 13:2-5).

Here we learn that he was born to a mother who, formerly, could not bear children — a miracle birth. As a Danite, he was a product of Rachel's contrivance to bear children through her handmaid, Bilhah:

"And when Rachel saw that she bare Jacob no children, Rachel envied her sister; and said unto Jacob, Give me children, or else I die.

"And Jacob's anger was kindled against Rachel: and he said, Am I in God's stead, who hath withheld from thee the fruit of the womb?

"And she said, Behold my maid Bilhah, go in unto her; and she shall bear upon my knees, that I may also have children by her.

"And she gave him Bilhah her handmaid to wife: and Jacob

went in unto her.

"And Bilhah conceived, and bare Jacob a son.

"And Rachel said, God hath judged me, and hath also heard my voice, and hath given me a son: therefore called she his name Dan" (Genesis 30:1-6).

Just as Sarai had used her handmaid, Hagar, to produce a son, Rachel repeated the mistake — through her handmaid, Bilhah. Samson is the result of Rachel's attempt to produce a messiah by a surrogate mother. Let us note that Moses chose two men to head up the work of building the tabernacle — Bezaleel of the tribe of Judah and Aholiab of the tribe of Dan. A rivalry developed between Dan and Judah over who would produce the Messiah, continues throughout the Scriptures. The snake, a symbol of Satan, became the mascot of the tribe of Dan. On his deathbed, Jacob said:

"Dan shall judge his people, as one of the tribes of Israel.

"Dan shall be a serpent by the way, an adder in the path, that biteth the horse heels, so that his rider shall fall backward" (Genesis 49:16,17).

Moses said of the tribe:

"Dan is a lion's whelp: he shall leap from Bashan" (Deuteronomy 33:22).

What Happened to Dan?

The territory of Bashan is located north of the Sea of Galilee near the Labanon border. Though Dan was originally given land southwest of Jerusalem, the Philistines deprived the tribe of their inheritance. Samson failed to secure it. The Danites were forced to move north — to the very territory prophesied by Moses. By the time of David, however, the tribe had evacuated their cities in the area of Bashan. The first eight chapters of I Chronicles gives a brief history of the other tribes, leaving out Dan. The tribe had disappeared. To this day, they are called, "the lost tribe."

It appears that they may have traveled to the islands of southern Greece and established the Spartan Empire. Early Greek accounts tell of one, Danaus, who came by boat from Phoenicia with his fifty daughters (the *Danades*) to become king of the island nation. At first they were known by the name "*Danaans*." Homer, the Greek historian, uses the term *Danaans* throughout his *Iliad* and *Odyssey*, for the tribe who eventually became known as the Lacedemonians and later, Spartans. In the second century B.C., a letter from the Lacedemonian king, Areus, was sent to Onais, the high priest in Jerusalem, claiming kinship to the Jews:

"It has been discovered in a document concerning the Lacedemonians and the Jews that they are brothers, and are of the race of Abraham" (I Maccabees 12:20,21). The first-century Jewish historian, Flavius Josephus, referred to these people as Spartans, but in his inclusion of the above epistle, he also used the term Lacedemonians:

"We have met with a certain writing, whereby we have discovered that both the Jews and the Lacedemonians are of one stock, and are derived from the kindred of Abraham. It is but just, therefore, that you, who are our brethren, should send to us about any of your concerns as you please. We will also do the same thing, and esteem your concerns as our own, and will look upon our concerns as in common with yours. Demotoles, who brings you this letter, will bring your answer back to us. This letter is four-square; and the symbol is an eagle, with a dragon in his claws" (*Antiquities* XII,II).

The symbol of the Spartans, an eagle and dragon, were the identical symbols ascribed to the tribe of Dan. The Spartan letter was brought to Jerusalem a few years before the Syrian invasion and desecration of the temple by Antiochus IV Epiphanes. Several years later, after the death of Antiochus IV, Jonathan, brother of Judas Macabbeus, sent a letter to the Spartans to renew that earlier fraternal friendship. Josephus writes:

"Jonathan the high priest, the senate of the nation, the priests, and the rest of the Jewish people, to the Lacedemonians their brothers send greetings. In the past a letter was sent to Onias, the high priest from Aerus, one of your kings, stating that you are indeed our brothers, as the copy subjoined attests. Onias received the envoy with honor, and accepted the letter, in which a clear reference was made to friendship and alliance. For our part, though we have no need of these, having the consolation of the holy books in our possession. We venture to send, to renew our fraternal friendship with you, so that we may not become strangers to you, for a long time has elapsed since you sent us the letter. We may say that constantly on every occasion, at our festivals and on other appointed days, we make a remembrance of you in the sacrifices we offer and in our prayers, as it is right and fitting to remember brothers."

By the days of Josephus in first century, these ancient Danaans (Lacedemonians) were known as Spartans. Could they be the lost tribe of Dan?

In an apocryphal writing, *The Testaments of the Twelve Patriarchs*, dating back to at least 150 B.C., the dying Dan, like Jacob before him, gathered his children around his bed and prophesied about what the future held for his progeny. Among his predictions was this statement: "I read in the Book of Enoch, the Righteous, that your prince is Satan...." This led Jewish scholars to link the tribe of Dan with the Antichrist. Furthermore, Dan said, "I know that in the last days you will defect from the Lord, you will be offended at Levi, and revolt against Judah; but you will not prevail over them." Concerning this deathbed testament, a commentator concluded: "Dan prophesied to them ... that they would go astray from God's Law, that they would be estranged from their inheritance, from the race of Israel, and from their patrimony; and that is what occurred."

In the book of Revelation (chapter 7), Dan is missing from a list of the tribes. Yet, his symbol — a dragon — is included. It appears that the Antichrist may rise out of Israel's lost tribe. Like Samson, this pretender to the throne will bring the world to Armageddon. Though, for the most part, Samson typifies Israel, he also draws our attention to the man the world has been waiting for.

Raised as a Nazarite

Samson was called to be a Nazarite. Three prohibitions were placed upon his life. He was not allowed to cut his hair, touch any dead animal, or drink wine.

He was given an opportunity to fulfill his calling and utterly failed. He broke all three commandments. In like manner, the nation of Israel was set apart by Divine appointment to observe certain strict ordinances. But alas, the nation failed in every detail. It is uncanny to consider the parallels between the life of Samson and the history of Israel.

His Gentile Bride

In Judges, chapter 14, we are told of the first dilemma surrounding Samson. He set about to take a Gentile bride.

"And Samson went down to Timnath, and saw a woman in Timnath of the daughters of the Philistines.

"And he came up, and told his father and his mother, and said, I have seen a woman in Timnath of the daughters of the Philistines: now therefore get her for me to wife.

"Then his father and his mother said unto him, Is there never a woman among the daughters of thy brethren, or among all my people, that thou goest to take a wife of the uncircumcised Philistines? And Samson said unto his father, Get her for me; for she pleaseth me well.

"But his father and his mother knew not that it was of the LORD, that he sought an occasion against the Philistines: for at that time the Philistines had dominion over Israel" (Judges 14:1-4).

At this point, Samson appears as a messiah figure — taking a Gentile bride. But his motives are different from that of the true Messiah. He has no love for her. He only seeks an excuse to stir up trouble with the Philistines.

He Touches a Dead Lion

On the way to her house, he goes through a vineyard, encounters a lion and kills it with his bare hands. Why are we told that he traveled through a vineyard? Because he was forbidden to drink wine. Passing through the vineyard probably violated the covenant. Sometime later, as he went to fetch his bride for the wedding, he noticed that a swarm of bees had made honey in the lion's carcass:

"And after a time he returned to take her, and he turned aside to see the carcass of the lion: and, behold, there was a swarm of bees and honey in the carcass of the lion.

"And he took thereof in his hands, and went on eating, and came to his father and mother, and he gave them, and they did eat: but he told not them that he had taken the honey out of the carcass of the lion" (Judges 14:8,9).

Samson ate some of the contaminated honey, thus defiling himself and breaking his Nazarite vow by touching the carcass of the dead lion. Then he proceded to the wedding feast. It was the custom to drink wine at such feasts. Though the story does not explicitly say that he drank wine, he did travel through the vineyards of Timnath. Furthermore, the Hebrew word for feast, *"misteh,"* implies a drinking bout, which the Philistines would have enjoyed.

Though the Bible does not specifically say that Samson drank, the clear implication is that he did, and thereby broke his Nazarite vow. By this time, he was defiled, having broken two of the three prohibitions.

The Riddle of the Ages

During the wedding feast he proposed a riddle to his guests concerning the lion and the honey:

"And Samson said unto them, I will now put forth a riddle unto you: if ye can certainly declare it me within the seven days of the feast, and find it out, then I will give you thirty sheets and thirty change of garments:

"But if ye cannot declare it me, then shall ye give me thirty sheets and thirty change of garments. And they said unto him, Put forth thy riddle, that we may hear it.

"And he said unto them, Out of the eater came forth meat, and out of the strong came forth sweetness. And they could not in three days expound the riddle" (Judges 14:12-14).

The riddle appears to have prophetic overtones. The lion is a metaphor for Judah, the tribe chosen to produce the Messiah. The bees appear to be a cryptic metaphor for the Danites. The untold implication is that Dan will kill Judah and produce the honey of utopia in its carcass. According to Greek literature, the Spartans were known as the "people of the bear." They used honey in their pagan rituals. Also, the bee is a Babylonian symbol of *Debar*, the Hebrew term for "Word" — another metaphor of the Messiah. The riddle was seemingly saying, "Replace the Jewish lion with the Danite bee. Dan will produce the messianic 'Word' of God."

Furthermore, the Babylonian symbol of a lion with a bee in its mouth portrayed Mythra, sun god of Babylon. Making honey in the carcass of the lion was another way of portraying Mystery Babylon's part in the end-time.

By the third day of the week-long festival, the guests conspired with Samson's bride to trick him into disclosing the riddle. Samson told her the riddle, but not the answer. She told the guests and on the seventh day of the feast, they repeated the riddle to Samson:

"... they could not in three days expound the riddle
"And the men of the city said unto him on the seventh day before the sun went down, What is sweeter than honey? and what is stronger than a lion? And he said unto them, If ye had not plowed with my heifer, ye had not found out my riddle. (Judges 14:14,18).

The third and seventh days spoken of here may be indicative of the third and seventh millennia. Samson's riddle was devised in the third millennium. The Messianic Kingdom is due to come in the seventh millennium. In the ritual using the ashes of the red heifer, an unclean person was commanded to be sprinkled on the third day and on the seventh day:

"And the clean person shall sprinkle upon the unclean on the third day, and on the seventh day: and on the seventh day he shall purify himself, and wash his clothes, and bathe himself in water, and shall be clean at even" (Numbers 19:19).

The heifer used in the sacrifice was forbidden to pull a plow. Such a thing would make the heifer unfit for sacrifice:

"This is the ordinance of the law which the LORD hath commanded, saying, Speak unto the children of Israel, that they bring thee a red heifer without spot, wherein is no blemish, and upon which never came yoke" (Numbers 19:2).

Samson's declaration that his guests had *"plowed with his heifer"* has powerful prophetic overtones. Like a disqualified heifer, Samson's Gentile bride was found to be unfit. She had disclosed the riddle to his guests. They repeated the riddle, but not its underlying meaning. It is a riddle that will remain unresolved until the seventh millennium. Samson was so angry, he went to Ashkelon, slew thirty men, took their clothes, and paid his wager to the wedding guests. Then he went back to his father's home without his wife.

Some time later, when his temper had cooled down, Samson went to fetch his wife and found out that her father had given her to his best friend. Angered again, Samson caught 300 foxes, tied torches to their tails, and sent them through the cornfields of the Philistines.

Samson's bees represent a Danite pretender to the throne of Israel, who will attempt to create world utopia in the seventh millennium. Samson is also typical of Israel. New Testament Christianity, a Gentile bride, has been given to Israel's best friend, the Lord Jesus Christ. Like Samson, Israel killed the Lion of Judah. In the killing of the lion, Samson rendered himself unclean. In like manner, through the death of Jesus Christ, the nation of Israel was defiled.

In the story, Samson fell in love with Delilah, who

betrayed him and cut his hair. At this point, Samson was completely defiled. He had gone through the vineyards of Timnath, defiling himself with the fruit of the vine; he had killed a young lion in the vineyard, and had later retrieved some honey from it, defiling himself by touching a dead animal; and now he had revealed the secret of his power. He had allowed his hair to be cut, thus defiling himself — breaking the third and final commandment which was supposed to characterize his life.

When Samson lost his hair, he lost the spiritual source of his power. This is typical of Israel, who, having been defiled, lost it's glory and power.

Samson was blinded and made to push a millstone among the Gentiles for the rest of his life. In like manner, the Jewish people were spiritually blinded and scattered from their land. The "wandering Jew" has been made to live and work among the nations for the past two millennia. In the end, however, Samson, though blinded, regained his strength for one last big push. He was brought into the arena of the Philistines that they might make sport of him.

In the story, Samson entertained his enemies, after which he was allowed to rest. He asked the lad (who led him by the hand) to take him to the two middle pillars which supported the roof of the arena. Taking hold of the pillars, he prayed that he might be allowed to make amends for his wasted life, then pushed them over, collapsing the arena and killing 3,000 Philistines. Samson died that day, but he took as many of his enemies with him as he could:

"And Samson said, Let me die with the Philistines. And he bowed himself with all his might; and the house fell upon the lords, and upon all the people that were therein. So the dead which he slew at his death were more than they which he slew in his life" (Judges 16:30).

Samson's over-all ministry lasted twenty years. Most of that time was spent in captivity. In like manner, the Jewish people have spent twenty centuries among the nations since defiling themselves and killing the Lion of the tribe of Judah.

At the end of this age, Israel, though blinded, will regain its power for one last, big push — Armageddon. No wonder then, it is said of Israel, that she has a "Samson complex." The story of Samson is a prophecy presently being fulfilled in the life of Israel.

The Number Three

There is something else about the story of Samson which seems to stand out. That is the use of the number three. There must be a special reason why three is used continually throughout the story of his life. For instance, before his birth, the angel commanded that he be a Nazarite involving three prohibitions: (1) drinking wine; (2) touching anything unclean; and (3) cutting his hair.

Three times the injunction was repeated and each time it was addressed to his mother. The boy was to be so completely consecrated that his mother had to refrain from these things while he was in her womb.

The repetitions were clearly purposeful to leave the reader with no uncertainty regarding the theme of the story. The entire narrative of his life was centered around his breaking those three prohibitions.

He became involved with three women — his fiancee at Timnath; a harlot at Gaza; and the infamous Delilah.

Samson's use of the term *"heifer,"* is also noteworthy. The heifer was required to be at least in its third year at the time of its sacrifice.

At his wedding feast, he proposed a riddle to thirty guests (a multiple of three). When they had him tricked into revealing the riddle, he became angry, went to Ashkelon, killed thirty men, took their clothes and paid his debt. Later, he tied firebrands to the tails of 300 foxes and burned the cornfields of the Philistines (a multiple of three). Because of his arson, 3,000 of his Jewish brethren came to arrest him (another multiple of three).

Finally, on the last day of his life, he pushed over the pillars that supported the arena and 3,000 Philistines died in the collapse of the building.

Because of the story's overwhelming preoccupation with the number three, I consulted the book, *"Number in Scripture"* by E. W. Bullinger, to find out what was so significant about the number three:

"In this number we have quite a new set of phenomena. We come to the first geometrical figure. Two straight lines cannot possibly enclose any space, or form a plane figure; neither can two plane surfaces form a solid. Three lines are necessary to form a plane figure; and three dimensions of length, breadth, and height, are necessary to form a solid. Hence, three is the symbol of the cube — the simplest form of solid figure. As two is the symbol of the square, or plane contents, so three is the symbol of the cube, or solid contents. Three, therefore, stands for that which is solid, real, substantial, complete, and entire."

A blueprint only offers two dimensions: length and width. The drawing of an object merely illustrates design. However, when the third dimension is added, it is taken off of the drawing board and put into reality. Three offers a completion to that which is planned.

The great laver which stood in front of Solomon's Temple held 3,000 baths of water, each bath consisting of five gallons. Five is the number of grace and 3,000 represents the fullness of that brazen laver. Furthermore, that great brazen laver was supported by twelve oxen — three looking north, three looking west, three looking south, and three looking east. It is indicative of the Great Commission. Our Savior commanded us to go into all the world and preach the Gospel to every creature. On the Day of Pentecost 3,000 people were baptized, again showing the fulfillment of the plan of God. Our conclusion is that the number three marks the fullness and completion of God's plan of the ages.

Samson was not a total failure, because in the end, he accomplished his task — bringing judgment upon a wicked and unbelieving people. Their number, 3,000, is symbolic of the completed group of unbelievers at the end of the age. Therefore, Samson's involvement with the number three is associated with God's plan for mankind. A blinded but restored Israel will finally bring down the judgment of God upon an unbelieving world.

Chapter Thirteen

Samuel
Son of Grace

Samuel had the distinct honor of having two Old Testament books named after him — I & II Samuel. He was the fourteenth and last of the judges — bridging Israel's historic transition to the monarchy. During his administration, he anointed two kings, Saul and David and is listed in the New Testament book of Hebrews as one of the great heroes of the faith:

*"And what shall I more say? for the time would fail me to tell of Gideon, and of Barak, and of Samson, and of Jephthae; of David also, and **Samuel** …"* (Hebrews 11:32).

There is more to the life of Samuel than one might determine at first glance. Hannah (whose name means "grace") prayed for a son. Her husband, Elkanah (meaning "whom God creates") produced this son through Hannah (grace) and called him, Samuel (meaning "God hears"). This teaches the very essence of grace. We do not receive salvation because we work for it or deserve it, but because we ask — and God hears our prayers. The Hebrew term, Samuel, also can be translated as "renowned" — implying that people were impressed with his demeanor. He was a messiah figure — a symbolic type of Christ. His miracle birth and renowned appearance were prophetically typical of the Savior.

Born of a Barren Mother

Samuel's was a miracle birth. His mother, Hannah, was barren. However, at the tabernacle one day, she prayed earnestly for a child:

> *"And she was in bitterness of soul, and prayed unto the LORD, and wept sore."*
>
> *"And she vowed a vow, and said, O LORD of hosts, if thou wilt indeed look on the affliction of thine handmaid, and remember me, and not forget thine handmaid, but wilt give unto thine handmaid a man child, then I will give him unto the LORD all the days of his life, and there shall no razor come upon his head"* (I Samuel 1:10,11).

Hannah joins the list of other barren women in the Bible, divinely chosen to demonstrate the future birth of the Messiah. In our study on *"Symbols of the Red Heifer"* we discussed how Sarah, Rebekah, Rachel and Samson's mother also help to draw a prophetic picture of God's plan for the birth of His Divine Son. Christ had to be the firstborn son of a virgin. There must be no doubt that the "seed" promised to Eve (Genesis 3:15) would not be the product of man. From the early pages of the Bible, it is apparent that God was laying a prophetic scenario for the birth of His own Son. Those women helped to demonstrate the plan that was later predicted by Isaiah:

"Behold, a virgin shall conceive, and bear a son, and shall call His name Immanuel" (Isaiah 7:14).

Isaac, Jacob, Joseph, Samson and Samuel were messiah figures that demonstrated the Savior's divinely orchestrated birth.

Upon weaning her son, Hannah brought Samuel to the Tabernacle at Shiloh for his dedication to a life of divine service. Like Samson, the child was devoted to a Nazarite vow — a razor would never touch his hair. He was to be the antithesis of Samson, the failed messiah figure that preceded him.

The Servant Lamp

A comparison of dates between Samuel and Samson reveals a relationship between the two stories. According to the *Open Bible*, Samson was born in 1100 B.C. and died around 1060 B.C. He judged Israel for twenty years. It is assumed that Samson was about twenty years old when he set out to marry a Philistine woman from Timnath. He died at about age forty. Samuel was born around 1070 B.C., during the years of Samson's work. Samuel would have been about ten years old when Samson died. This comparison of the times may help us to understand a statement woven into the story of God's call to Samuel. The child laid down one night and heard the voice of God calling to him. This event took place shortly before problems developed with the center lamp of the Tabernacle Menorah:

*"And ere the **lamp of God** went out in the temple of the LORD, where the ark of God was, and Samuel was laid down to sleep;*

"That the LORD called Samuel: and he answered, Here am I" (I Samuel 3:3,4).

If Samuel was about ten years old when this event took place, then Samson's blindness and death was imminent. According to the system of dates given in the *Open Bible*, Samuel's encounter with God took place around 1060 B.C., the very year ascribed to the betrayal, blindness and death of Samson. Perhaps the middle lamp on the seven golden candlesticks went out upon either his blindness or death. Samson (meaning "child of the sun") was the fourth of seven men born of six barren women and one virgin. Chronologically, Samson represented the servant lamp. His blindness and subsequent death took place around the same time that the servant lamp failed. It seems likely that there was a connection between those events. In observing the following prayer of praise offered by Hannah, note that she spoke about seven sons who would be borne of barren women:

"They that were full have hired out themselves for bread; and they that were hungry ceased: so that the barren hath borne seven; and she that hath many children is waxed feeble" (I Samuel 2:5).

Though Hannah was only the fifth of six barren women and one virgin, she predicted there would be two more. Those would eventually be the barren Elizabeth, mother of John the Baptist, and the virgin Mary, mother of Jesus.

The Ark of the Covenant

Before observing Hannah's prayer of praise, let us review the early life of Samuel. He was given to the Lord and raised by Eli's family. Each year, Hannah would bring new clothes for her growing son. When Samuel was about ten years old, he had a nighttime encounter with God. The lad was told that Eli's wicked sons would be killed. About ten years later, Israel was embroiled in a battle with the Philistines at a place called Ebenezer. Hophni and Phinehas accompanied the Ark of the Covenant out into the midst of a battle with the Philistines and were killed. Israel's enemy took the Ark and kept it about seven months, during which time they were severely judged by God. This probably took place around 1050 B.C., as Samuel was approaching the age of twenty. This was also the time when Eli died and Eleazar became the High Priest.

The Philistines placed the Holy Ark in the temple of Dagon, their fish god. The next morning, Dagon was found fallen before the Ark. On the following morning, Dagon was found broken before the Ark. The Philistines fell sick in the presence of the Ark. Eventually, it was moved from city to city, until all of the Philistines were sick.

It was finally placed in an open field. We are told that mice emerged from the ground and devoured their crops. After seven months of punishment, the Philistines decided to send the Ark back to Israel.

Upon its arrival near the town of *Beth-Shemesh*, the Israelites gathered to examine it. The crowd that stood nearby died with those who violated the sanctity of the Ark. Finally, it was taken to *Kirjath-Jearim*, to the home of Abinadab, whose son, Eleazar, became the guardian of the Ark.

The Meeting at Mizpeh

Samuel called for a meeting of the men of Israel at *Mizpeh* to observe the return of the Ark and renew their religious vows. *Mizpeh* means "a watch tower, a tower used for military purposes." It was there that Samuel offered sacrifices to the Lord. The Philistines heard that the Israelites were preoccupied with religious activity and decided to attack:

"And as Samuel was offering up the burnt offering, the Philistines drew near to battle against Israel: but the LORD thundered with a great thunder on that day upon the Philistines, and discomfited them; and they were smitten before Israel" (I Samuel 7:10).

Samuel called upon God for protection and a sudden thunderstorm smote the enemy. This was Samuel's first recorded official act as Israel's new judge. What happened that day fulfilled a prophecy given in Hannah's prayer of praise on the day she brought her young son to serve the Lord:

"The adversaries of the LORD shall be broken to pieces; out of heaven shall he thunder upon them ... " (I Samuel 2:10).

The Lord brought a supernatural judgment upon the invading armies and we are reminded of the great hail storm with its graphic description of God's judgment during the future battle of Armageddon:

"And there fell upon men a great hail out of heaven, every stone about the weight of a talent: and men blasphemed God because of the plague of the hail; for the plague thereof was exceeding great" (Revelation 16:21).

Here is the ultimate fulfillment of that ancient prophecy illustrated in the battle at *Mizpeh*. It appears to be prophetic of the Tribulation Period when Israel will gather at the symbolic *Mizpeh* (a watch tower) to prepare for that final battle. Though the situation will offer little hope, it will be a day of victory for Israel.

Samuel became the fourteenth and final judge. He ruled in the office of a potentate without a formal title. It was understood that only the Lord was King in Israel — until the day the elders demanded that Samuel anoint a king.

Samuel and the Song of Moses

Now let us return to the infancy of Samuel and review Hannah's prayer of praise. It closely follows a similar theme given in the Song of Moses. Quotes from the Song of Moses are emphasized (bold) in Hannah's prayer:

"And Hannah prayed, and said, My heart rejoiceth in the LORD, mine horn is exalted in the LORD; my mouth is enlarged over mine enemies; because I rejoice in thy salvation.

"There is none holy as the LORD: for there is none beside thee: neither is there any rock like our God.

"Talk no more so exceeding proudly; let not arrogancy come out of your mouth: for the LORD is a God of knowledge, and

by him actions are weighed.

"The bows of the mighty men are broken, and they that stumbled are girded with strength.

"They that were full have hired out themselves for bread; and they that were hungry ceased: so that the barren hath borne seven; and she that hath many children is waxed feeble.

"The LORD killeth, and maketh alive: he bringeth down to the grave, and bringeth up.

"The LORD maketh poor, and maketh rich: he bringeth low, and lifteth up.

"He raiseth up the poor out of the dust, and lifteth up the beggar from the dunghill, to set them among princes, and to make them inherit the throne of glory: for the pillars of the earth are the LORD'S, and he hath set the world upon them.

"He will keep the feet of his saints, and the wicked shall be silent in darkness; for by strength shall no man prevail.

"The adversaries of the LORD shall be broken to pieces; out of heaven shall he thunder upon them: the LORD shall judge the ends of the earth; and he shall give strength unto his king, and exalt the horn of his anointed" (I Samuel 2:1-10).

Hannah's prayer follows a theme given in the *Song of Moses*. For example when she said, *"mine horn is exalted ..."* she was probably referring to Psalm 92:10 which says, *"... my horn shalt thou exalt."* When she said, *"... I rejoice in thy salvation"* she was probably referring to Psalm 95:1 which says, *"Let us make a joyful noise to the rock of our salvation."* She made a reference to the *"rock"* as she said, *"... neither is there any rock like our God."* When she said, *"... the Lord is a God of knowledge,"* she was probably referring to Psalm 94:11 which says, *"The LORD knoweth the thoughts of man...."* When she said, *"The bows of the mighty men are broken,"* she was probably referring to Psalm 94:23 which says, "... *he shall bring upon them their own iniquity, and shall cut them off in their own wickedness; yea, the LORD our God shall cut them off.*"

When she said, "*The LORD killeth and maketh alive,*" she seemed to be referring to Deuteronomy 32:39 which says, "... *I kill, and I make alive....*" When she said, "*He raiseth up the poor ... to set them among princes*" she was probably referring to Deuteronomy 32:43 which says, "... *he will avenge the blood of his servants ... and will be merciful unto his land, and to his people.*" When she said, "... *the Lord shall judge the ends of the earth*" she may have been referring to Psalm 96:13 which says, "... *he cometh to judge the earth....*"

Psalm 99

Somehow, Samuel became associated with the *Song of Moses*. We find his name recorded alongside Moses and Aaron in the eleventh stanza of Moses' song — Psalm 99:

> "*Moses and Aaron among his priests, and Samuel among them that call upon his name; they called upon the LORD, and he answered them.*
> "*He spake unto them in the cloudy pillar...*" (Psalm 99:6,7).

We are not certain as to how Samuel's name was made a part of the *Song of Moses*. However, I think we can determine why it is there. We are told in the Bible that the *shekinah* glory resided above the tabernacle in the wilderness. It appeared as a column of cloud and fire ascending above the Holy of holies.

Rabbis say that this same glory also appeared above the home of Samuel. They suggest that is the reason Samuel's name is included in Psalm 99. The psalm says that God *"... spake unto them in the cloudy pillar"* (Psalm 99:7).

Rabbinic commentaries say that Psalm 99 follows the meaning of Dan's name — judge:

"The king's strength also loveth judgment; thou dost establish equity, thou executest judgment and righteousness in Jacob" (Psalm 99:4).

The names of Moses, Aaron and Samuel in verse 6 speak of the Law, the priesthood and the prophets. Under Samuel's administration, the term "prophet" was institutionalized. Samuel was appointed head of Israel's first company of the prophets.

"... they saw the company of the prophets prophesying, and Samuel standing as appointed over them" (I Samuel 19:20).

In the book of Acts, Samuel is associated specifically with the prophets:

"Yea, and all the prophets from Samuel and those that follow after, as many as have spoken, have likewise foretold of these days" (Acts 3:24).

Here, he is mentioned as the one who introduced Israel's era of the prophets. In chapter 13, he is designated as a prophet that concluded the era of Israel's judges:

"And after that he gave unto them judges about the space of four hundred and fifty years, until Samuel the prophet" (Acts 13:20).

His inclusion in Psalm 99, dedicated to Dan, may

be a prophetic reference to the rise of the Antichrist. Early Jewish scholars believed Dan would produce the Antichrist. Since Samuel anointed Saul (a substitute king) and later David (the promised king), we may entertain the thought that Israel could someday choose a substitute messiah before the arrival of their true Messiah. We are not suggesting that the Antichrist should have appeared in 1999, but merely noting that the psalm implies the future arrival of such a man.

Saul, the Benjamite

Israel became resentful of the judges and demanded that Samuel anoint a king: *"... make us a king to judge us like all the nations"* (I Samuel 8:5). If only Israel had been willing to wait one more generation, God would have given them His promised monarch. David, being the tenth generation in the tribe of Judah, had a divine calling to sit upon Israel's throne. Judah was given the promise of kingship by the dying Jacob who said, *"The scepter shall not depart from Judah, nor a lawgiver from between his feet, until Shiloh come..."* (Genesis 49:10). Because the father of the tribe had committed adultery with his daughter-in-law, Tamar, and produced an illegitimate son, Pharez, the tribe was under the curse of the Mosaic Law which says, *"A bastard shall not enter into the congregation of the LORD; even to his tenth generation shall he not enter into the congregation of the Lord"* (Deuteronomy 23:2). David was that tenth generation. His genealogy is given in the last chapter of Ruth:

"Now these are the generations of Pharez: Pharez begat Hezron,

"And Hezron begat Ram, and Ram begat Amminadab,

"And Amminadab begat Nahshon, and Nahshon begat Salmon,

"And Salmon begat Boaz, and Boaz begat Obed,

"And Obed begat Jesse, and Jesse begat David" (Ruth 4:18-22).

David was not yet born when Samuel anointed Saul to be Israel's first king. If the people had only waited, they would have been blessed with God's best. However, the people were not willing to wait upon the promise of God. They demanded a king immediately. At this point, may we be reminded that the Orthodox Jews have been praying over the last few years for God to send the Messiah immediately. It is possible that in the place of the true Messiah, God will allow Israel to accept a substitute. This appears to be what happened in the case of Saul. He was a handsome man, standing head and shoulders above his peers. However, his reign is the story of one disaster after another.

Saul was from the tribe of Benjamin. Though some suggest that a messiah figure will come out of the tribe of Dan, there are others who think Israel's long-awaited messiah will be from Benjamin. In a book entitled, *Holy Blood, Holy Grail*, Michael Baigent and associates claim that Jesus survived the crucifixion, married Mary Magdalene and produced sacred children who eventually sired the royalty of Europe. They suggest that Mary Magdalene was from the lineage of Benjamin, linking her with Martha and Lazarus, who lived in Bethany, a town on the eastern slope of the Mount of Olives in the territory which belonged to the tribe of Benjamin. Concerning Benjamin, they wrote, "Most Benjamites did go into exile. Their exile supposedly took them to Greece, to the central Pelopponesus — to Arcadia, in short, where they supposedly became aligned with the Arcadian royal line. Toward the advent of the Christian era they are then said to have migrated up the Danube and the Rhine, intermarrying with certain Teutonic tribes and eventually engendering the Sicambrian Franks — the immediate forebears of the Merovingians" (*Holy Blood*, p. 274). May I quickly but briefly say, I do not believe in their theory. For more information on this subject, I suggest you read my book, *Guardians of the Grail*. It is interesting, however, to note that Saul, like Samson before him, was a messiah figure who failed to live up to the expectations of the people.

Saul's Selfish Sacrifice

Soon after Saul became the king, he was confronted by an enormous Philistine army. They had amassed their troops at Michmash, just east of Bethaven. Saul went to Gilgal to await word from Samuel, who had promised to come in seven days. On the evening of the seventh day, with no sight of Samuel, the king took upon himself to offer the sacrifice. Within a short time after the sacrifice, Samuel came. When the man of God found out that King Saul had usurped the office of the prophet, he was angry and said,

"... thou hast done foolishly: thou hast not kept the com-
mandment of the LORD thy God, which he commanded
thee: for now would the LORD have established thy king-
dom upon Israel for ever.
"But now thy kingdom shall not continue" (I Samuel
13:13,14).

This action by Saul smacks of the abomination of
desolation which will one day be perpetrated by another failed messiah figure — the Antichrist.

Agag, the Amalekite

The final straw that broke the proverbial camel's
back came when Saul led the Israelites into battle
against the Amalekites. Samuel had told him to
slaughter all members of the tribe. The king was not
to leave a soul alive:

"Now go and smite Amalek, and utterly destroy all that they
have, and spare them not; but slay both man and woman, infant
and suckling, ox and sheep, camel and ass" (I Samuel 15:3).

King Saul did not obey the command of the Lord.
He spared Agag, their king. Saul should have killed
the king, the people, their cattle and flocks. However, he spared the sheep and the king. When Samuel
heard the bleating of the sheep, he asked him:

"... what meaneth then this bleating of the sheep in mine
ears, and the lowing of the oxen which I hear?" (I Samuel
15:14).

No explanation would suffice. Saul had failed.
Samuel declared that Saul's administration was
doomed. God withdrew His Spirit from the king and
allowed a demon to torture him. This prophetic sce-

nario will also be fulfilled in the Antichrist, who will be possessed by the devil, after having been loved and revered by Israel and the world. His future reign, like Saul's, will be filled with one disaster after another. Perhaps we could call it poetic justice that Saul died at the hands of an Amalekite.

The Anointing of David

Samuel had one more major accomplishment to undertake. God called upon him to anoint a successor to Saul:

"And the LORD said unto Samuel, How long wilt thou mourn for Saul, seeing I have rejected him from reigning over Israel? fill thine horn with oil, and go, I will send thee to Jesse the Bethlehemite: for I have provided me a king among his sons.

"And Samuel said, How can I go? if Saul hear it, he will kill me. And the LORD said, Take an heifer with thee, and say, I am come to sacrifice to the LORD.

"And call Jesse to the sacrifice, and I will show thee what thou shalt do: and thou shalt anoint unto me him whom I name unto thee" (I Samuel 16:1-3).

We will deal at length with this story in our study on the life of David. Also, we have addressed this particular occasion in our study on the ritual of the red heifer. Therefore, we shall only observe prophetic aspects of Samuel's ministry in this chapter. Since this was the final major story given about Samuel before his death, we may assume that its prophetic significance reaches into the far future — to the end-time. Two things are important about this event — the sacrifice of a red heifer and the anointing of

David. Presently, religious Jews are looking for a tenth red heifer for sacrifice. An ancient rabbinical commentary says that the tenth heifer will be a harbinger of the coming of the Messiah. The anointing of David is symbolic of the anointing of his future offspring, who is prophesied to be Israel's Messiah. Samuel's epic event directs our attention to present-day Israel and the anticipation of Messiah's arrival.

Samuel looked at the first seven sons and was not satisfied in his spirit. He asked Jesse if he had yet another son, to which the Bethlehemite replied:

"... there remaineth yet the youngest, and, behold, he keepeth the sheep. And Samuel said unto Jesse, Send and fetch him: for we will not sit down till he come hither" (I Samuel 16:11).

David was the eighth son of Jesse. The first seven, a spiritually perfect number, would not do. It took the eighth, the number of new beginning, to produce Israel's greatest king. It is interesting to note that the numerical value of Jesus (Greek) is 888. It seems that every detail has prophetic overtones. Samuel poured the anointing oil upon the head of David, completed his sacrifice and returned to Ramah where he spent the remainder of his days.

David Flees to Samuel

David was eventually given Michal, Saul's daughter, for a wife. But Saul's increasing suspicions against David led the king to attempt to kill him. David fled and came to Samuel for protection:

*"So David fled, and escaped, and came to Samuel to Ramah, and told him all that Saul had done to him. And he and Samuel went and dwelt in **Naioth**"* (I Samuel 19:18).

Naioth [ניות] refers to a "home or habitation." It is assumed that Samuel received David into his own home in the city of Ramah. It was the home where rabbis say the *shekinah* glory dwelt. In certain respects, that is where Jesus is today. When Saul came to arrest him, the king fell under the power of God and could not accomplish his fiendish task.

Samuel's Death

Just before the death of Samuel, David had an encounter with Saul. It was here that the king acknowledged that David was divinely ordained to succeed him upon Israel's throne:

"And now, behold, I know well that thou shalt surely be king, and that the kingdom of Israel shall be established in thine hand.

"Swear now therefore unto me by the LORD, that thou wilt not cut off my seed after me, and that thou wilt not destroy my name out of my father's house.

"And David sware unto Saul. And Saul went home; but David and his men gat them up unto the hold" (I Samuel 24:20-22).

What Saul had previously denied, he now admits. Could this be prophetic of Israel's denial of Christ? Will the end of suffering come only when the Jews admit that Jesus really is their Messiah and that He deserves to rule over them? Saul finally recognizes David's right to the throne. With that fact established, the old prophet could rest in peace:

"And Samuel died; and all the Israelites were gathered to-gether, and lamented him, and buried him in his house at **Ramah***. And David arose, and went down to the wilderness of Paran"* (I Samuel 25:1).

Samuel was buried in his home at *Ramah*. The dwelling would never be occupied by another. It would become a memorial to the memory of a great prophet — one so great, the *shekinah* glory dwelt over his house. *Ramah* [רמה] means "height." It seems typical of heaven. There could be no better place for Samuel to dwell and later be interred.

Samuel's Return to Endor

On the night before King Saul died, he approached a witch at the village of Endor and asked her to bring Samuel back for one last consultation. I suspect she was as surprised as anyone when Samuel appeared. The message was one of doom for the king:

"And when the woman saw Samuel, she cried with a loud voice: and the woman spake to Saul, saying, Why hast thou deceived me? for thou art Saul.

"And the king said unto her, Be not afraid: for what sawest thou? And the woman said unto Saul, I saw gods ascending out of the earth.

"And he said unto her, What form is he of? And she said, An old man cometh up; and he is covered with a mantle. And Saul perceived that it was Samuel, and he stooped with his face to the ground, and bowed himself.

"And Samuel said to Saul, Why hast thou disquieted me, to bring me up? And Saul answered, I am sore distressed; for

the Philistines make war against me, and God is departed from me, and answereth me no more, neither by prophets, nor by dreams: therefore I have called thee, that thou mayest make known unto me what I shall do.

"Then said Samuel, Wherefore then dost thou ask of me, seeing the LORD is departed from thee, and is become thine enemy?

"And the LORD hath done to him, as he spake by me: for the LORD hath rent the kingdom out of thine hand, and given it to thy neighbor, even to David:

"Because thou obeyedst not the voice of the LORD, nor executedst his fierce wrath upon Amalek, therefore hath the LORD done this thing unto thee this day.

"Moreover the LORD will also deliver Israel with thee into the hand of the Philistines: and to morrow shalt thou and thy sons be with me: the LORD also shall deliver the host of Israel into the hand of the Philistines.

"Then Saul fell straightway all along on the earth, and was sore afraid, because of the words of Samuel: and there was no strength in him; for he had eaten no bread all the day, nor all the night" (I Samuel 28:12-20).

According to the Scripture, the woman described him as an old man covered in a mantle. We may assume that the soul of Samuel was alive and dwelling in Abraham's bosom. He appeared aged and wearing a tallit — the prayer shawl of the Jews. Also, he was enjoying a peaceful and quiet existence for he said, *"Why has thou disquieted me?"* Since the advent of Calvary, believers no longer live in Abraham's bosom, but are transported directly to heaven. However, the bliss of Abraham's bosom is enjoyed in that wonderful place to which we aspire to go. Those who have gone before us are happy and do not wish to return. We can see this in the attitude Samuel displayed.

One more thing. Samuel told Saul that he and his sons would be with him the next day. I must say, that is the essence of grace. Saul deserved much worse. Yet the wicked king joined Samuel in Abraham's bosom — to await the death, burial and resurrection of David's scion — Israel's Messiah! There is only one redemption for a life like Saul lived. That is the sacrifice of Jesus Christ on the cross. By the way, Saul was no worse than the rest of us when it comes to pleasing God. Isaiah put it quite well when he said, *"All we like sheep have gone astray...."* I would rather live my life like Samuel, but there is hope for people like Saul.

Chapter Fourteen

The First and Second Coming of David

The stories recorded in the Old Testament are more than mere historical accounts written to document the development of the human race. They offer more for us to learn than just the moral values evident in their telling. It is true that they contain examples of good versus evil. Certainly, we should learn how to conduct ourselves from them. Yet, there is more.

The stories of the Old Testament should not be compared with *Aesop's Fables* or *Mother Goose Rhymes*. They are not the mere product of human inspiration. They are divinely written in order to teach us about God's prophetic plan of the ages. A study of these ancient biographies actually reveals a complex pattern which lends support and evidence to the veracity of the Bible's great prophecies.

For example, the lives of David, Samson, Ruth, and Jonah offer prophetic insights about Israel — including the destruction of its cities; Jewish dispersion among the nations; a promised return; the war of Armageddon; and redemption by the Messiah.

Not only did the prophets Isaiah, Jeremiah, Ezekiel, Daniel, and others predict these events, but prophetic patterns, which reinforce these prophecies, emerge through the biographical sketches of Israel's ancient heroes.

Let us, therefore, examine the life of David and draw some prophetic parallels between those events recorded in his life and certain predictions made about Israel and their Messiah.

The Shepherd

The first account given of David reveals him as a young shepherd. The Lord tells Samuel that Saul is a failure and that he should go to Bethlehem, to the house of Jesse, and anoint one of his sons to be the next king of Israel. According to the story, Samuel is afraid. He tells the Lord that King Saul will kill him when he finds out what he has done:

"And the LORD said unto Samuel, How long wilt thou mourn for Saul, seeing I have rejected him from reigning over Israel? fill thine horn with oil, and go, I will send thee to Jesse the Bethlehemite: for I have provided me a king among his sons.

"And Samuel said, How can I go? if Saul hear it, he will kill me. And the LORD said, Take an heifer with thee, and say, I am come to sacrifice to the LORD.

"And call Jesse to the sacrifice, and I will show thee what

thou shalt do: and thou shalt anoint unto me him whom I name unto thee.

"And Samuel did that which the LORD spake, and came to Bethlehem. And the elders of the town trembled at his coming, and said, Comest thou peaceably?

"And he said, Peaceably: I am come to sacrifice unto the LORD: sanctify yourselves, and come with me to the sacrifice. And he sanctified Jesse and his sons, and called them to the sacrifice" (I Samuel 16:1-5).

The Red Heifer

Samuel was told to take a heifer — a young genetically pure female, completely red — a virgin which had never birthed a calf. The sacrifice of a red heifer was rare — only seven of them during the 1,500 years from Moses to Christ. Their ashes, mixed with water, were used to cleanse the sanctuary, its vessels, the very ground upon which it set, the priesthood, and all who came to worship.

At the time of the destruction of Herod's Temple in A.D. 70, the ashes — along with other implements for worship — were hidden away for a future generation. In recent years, several efforts have been made to discover the missing ashes. It is said that their discovery is necessary in order to reestablish the priesthood and build a new temple.

The particular sacrifice which took place at Bethlehem, under the direction of Samuel, is the only account given in the pages of the Old Testament — from the time the ordinance was given to Moses in Numbers 19. Therefore, this was a very special event.

According to the Lord's instructions, Samuel invites
the house of Jesse to assist him:

*"And it came to pass, when they were come, that he looked
on Eliab, and said, Surely the LORD's anointed is before him.*

*"But the LORD said unto Samuel, Look not on his counte-
nance, or on the height of his stature; because I have refused
him: for the LORD seeth not as man seeth; for man looketh
on the outward appearance, but the LORD looketh on the
heart.*

*"Then Jesse called Abinadab, and made him pass before
Samuel. And he said, Neither hath the LORD chosen this.*

*"Then Jesse made Shammah to pass by. And he said, Nei-
ther hath the LORD chosen this.*

*"Again, Jesse made seven of his sons to pass before Samuel.
And Samuel said unto Jesse, The LORD hath not chosen these.*

*"And Samuel said unto Jesse, Are here all thy children?
And he said, There remaineth yet the youngest, and, behold,
he keepeth the sheep. And Samuel said unto Jesse, Send
and fetch him: for we will not sit down till he come hither"*
(I Samuel 16:6-11).

As the story goes, Samuel takes one look at Eliab,
the eldest son of Jesse, and thinks that he must be
God's choice for the next king. Eliab's name means
"God of my fathers." Not so. God instructs Samuel
to look further, saying that men look upon the outward appearance, but that He looks upon the heart.

Of Jesse's eight sons, only Eliab, Abinadab and
Shammah are named here. Abinadab's name means
"father of nobility," while Shammah's name refers
to "desolation" or "waste." We shall see these three
again at the battle against Goliath.

After seven sons have passed before him, Samuel asked, *"Are here all thy children?"* He was not impressed with any of those. Jesse replies, *"There remaineth yet the youngest ... he keepeth the sheep."*

Even David's father did not have confidence in the future of his youngest son. He never dreamed that the boy could ever grow up to become a king! David was not Jesse's firstborn — a position reserved to the heir. He was just a son who kept the sheep:

"And he sent, and brought him in. Now he was ruddy, and withal of a beautiful countenance, and goodly to look to. And the LORD said, Arise, anoint him: for this is he.

"Then Samuel took the horn of oil, and anointed him in the midst of his brethren: and the spirit of the LORD came upon David from that day forward. So Samuel rose up, and went to Ramah" (I Samuel 16:12,13).

According to the Scripture, David had a ruddy complexion. Some have called it a reddish complexion. Flavius Josephus, the Jewish historian, took note that he had a yellow complexion — indicating the possibility that he had blond hair and a fair countenance. It appears that his skin was more susceptible to sunburn than it was to the browning effect of a suntan. It is rather interesting to note that the ancient *Book of Enoch* referred to Noah as having a fair countenance and light hair. Furthermore, there are two separate historical accounts, one recorded by Eusebius in the first century and another recorded by Gamaliel, which describe Jesus Christ as having a fair countenance, blue eyes, and blond hair. If so, the ruddy lad appears to be a striking picture of that one who is both the *"root and the offspring of David"* (Rev. 22:16).

Eight is the number of a new beginning. Therefore, David, the eighth son of Jesse, was an excellent choice for Israel's next king. The prophetic implication is evident. The numerical value of the Greek name of Jesus is 888. Obviously, Jesus is the one in view. Samuel anointed David with a special oil prepared for anointing kings. In like manner, the term, Christ, means "Anointed One." The spiritual application contained in this story points directly to Christ as the fulfillment of the prophecy.

The First Coming of David

The next time we see David, he is summoned by King Saul to play the harp in an effort to calm his troubled mind:

"But the spirit of the LORD departed from Saul, and an evil spirit from the LORD troubled him.

"And Saul's servants said unto him, Behold now, an evil spirit from God troubleth thee.

"Let our lord now command thy servants, which are before thee, to seek out a man, who is a cunning player on an harp: and it shall come to pass, when the evil spirit from God is upon thee, that he shall play with his hand, and thou shalt be well.

"And Saul said unto his servants, Provide me now a man that can play well, and bring him to me.

"Then answered one of the servants, and said, Behold, I have seen a son of Jesse the Bethlehemite, that is cunning in playing, and a mighty valiant man, and a man of war, and

prudent in matters, and a comely person, and the LORD is with him.

"Wherefore Saul sent messengers unto Jesse, and said, Send me David thy son, which is with the sheep.

"And Jesse took an ass laden with bread, and a bottle of wine, and a kid, and sent them by David his son unto Saul.

"And David came to Saul, and stood before him: and he loved him greatly; and he became his armourbearer.

"And Saul sent to Jesse, saying, Let David, I pray thee, stand before me; for he hath found favor in my sight.

"And it came to pass, when the evil spirit from God was upon Saul, that David took an harp, and played with his hand: so Saul was refreshed, and was well, and the evil spirit departed from him" (I Samuel 16:14-23).

Saul was so impressed that he wrote a letter to Jesse asking that David be allowed to stay for awhile and play the harp. For a short time, we do not know how long, David lived in the king's palace. He, who was a keeper of sheep, became a maker of music. This appears to be prophetic of the First Advent of Christ. He came the first time, not to fight, but to bring peace. Not only is Jesus our Great Shepherd, but He gives us eternal life. He puts a song in the heart and calms the troubled soul!

The Philistines Wage War

The Philistines lived along Israel's southern coast — territory that had been allocated for the tribe of Dan. Though the Danites were the largest among the tribes, they were given the smallest and most worthless land. Furthermore, no one offered to help the tribe rout out the Philistines. Eventually, the Danites were completely deprived of their inheritance and traveled north to the head-waters of the Jordan River — above Galilee at the foot of Mount Hermon. Jordan means "the going down of the Dan."

To this day, the Gaza area remains a thorn in the side of Israel. The modern name Palestine is a derivative from Philistia. It is also thought that the present-day Palestinians are descendants of the Philistines. In ancient days, they were a warrior tribe:

"Now the Philistines gathered together their armies to battle, and were gathered together at Shochoh, which belongeth to Judah, and pitched between Shochoh and Azekah, in Ephesdammin.

"And Saul and the men of Israel were gathered together, and pitched by the valley of Elah, and set the battle in array against the Philistines.

"And the Philistines stood on a mountain on the one side, and Israel stood on a mountain on the other side: and there was a valley between them" (I Samuel 17:1-3).

As the story progresses, David's three older brothers are conscripted to fight — Eliab, Abinadab and Shammah. David and the other four brothers must have been too young to become soldiers. Therefore, David returns home to keep his father's sheep:

"Now David was the son of that Ephrathite of Bethlehemjudah, whose name was Jesse; and he had eight sons: and the man went among men for an old man in the days of Saul.

"And the three eldest sons of Jesse went and followed Saul to the battle: and the names of his three sons that went to the

battle were Eliab the firstborn, and next unto him Abinadab, and the third Shammah.

"And David was the youngest: and the three eldest followed Saul.

"But David went and returned from Saul to feed his father's sheep at Bethlehem" (I Samuel 17:12-15).

May we be reminded that our Savior has returned to heaven where He cares for us — His Father's spiritual sheep. He, who was the *"Good Shepherd"* of John 10:11, has become the *"Great Shepherd"* of Hebrews 13:20. One day He will return to become the *"Chief Shepherd"* of I Peter 5:4:

*"I am the good shepherd: the **good shepherd** giveth his life for the sheep" (John 10:11).*

*"Now the God of peace, that brought again from the dead our Lord Jesus, that **great shepherd** of the sheep, through the blood of the everlasting covenant" (Hebrew 13:20).*

*"And when the **chief Shepherd** shall appear, ye shall receive a crown of glory that fadeth not away"* (I Peter 5:4).

Writing about the Messiah in Psalm 23, David exclaimed:

"The LORD is my shepherd; I shall not want.

"He maketh me to lie down in green pastures: he leadeth me beside the still waters.

"He restoreth my soul..." (Psalm 23:1-3).

David's duty among his father's sheep becomes a prophetic foreview of Christ.

Goliath Defies God

Now enters Goliath — who stands before Israel and defies their God for a period of forty days:

"And there went out a champion out of the camp of the Philistines, named Goliath, of Gath, whose height was six cubits and a span.

"And he had an helmet of brass upon his head, and he was armed with a coat of mail; and the weight of the coat was five thousand shekels of brass.

"And he had greaves of brass upon his legs, and a target of brass between his shoulders.

"And the staff of his spear was like a weaver's beam; and his spear's head weighed six hundred shekels of iron: and one bearing a shield went before him" (I Samuel 17:4-7).

Goliath stands for Armageddon — the giant of all wars. His measurements are strikingly similar to those of the Antichrist. He was over six cubits tall. His spear-head weighed six hundred shekels of iron. If he was like his brothers, he had six fingers on each hand and six toes on each foot! With so many sixes, how could he be anything else! He wages a war against Israel that prophetically typifies the future battle of Armageddon:

"And he stood and cried unto the armies of Israel, and said unto them, Why are ye come out to set your battle in array? am not I a Philistine, and ye servants to Saul? choose you a man for you, and let him come down to me.

"If he be able to fight with me, and to kill me, then will we be your servants: but if I prevail against him, and kill him, then shall ye be our servants, and serve us.

"And the Philistine said, I defy the armies of Israel this day; give me a man, that we may fight together.

"When Saul and all Israel heard those words of the Philistine, they were dismayed, and greatly afraid.

"And the Philistine drew near morning and evening, and presented himself forty days" (I Samuel 17:8-11,16).

Please note that Goliath challenged Israel for forty days. Now, one cannot say with certainty that those forty days represent a prophecy in times, but it is rather interesting that the term forty keeps occurring over and over again throughout the Scriptures. Forty is the number of testing. In this case, Israel was tested by Goliath.

We should also note that there are forty jubilee periods, of fifty years each, over a span of 2,000 years. Who knows? This may be an indication of the time between the First Advent of Christ and His return.

The Second Coming of David

We have observed the first advent of David as that part of the story when David played his harp before the disturbed king. Now we come to the second advent of David:

"And Jesse said unto David his son, Take now for thy brethren an ephah of this parched corn, and these ten loaves, and run to the camp to thy brethren;

"And carry these ten cheeses unto the captain of their thousand, and look how thy brethren fare, and take their pledge.

"Now Saul, and they, and all the men of Israel, were in the valley of Elah, fighting with the Philistines.

"And David rose up early in the morning, and left the sheep with a keeper, and took, and went, as Jesse had commanded him; and he came to the trench, as the host was going forth to the fight, and shouted for the battle.

"For Israel and the Philistines had put the battle in array, army against army" (I Samuel 17:17-21).

David leaves his father's sheep and travels to the site of the battle where he alone will volunteer to fight the giant, Goliath. One could call this the second coming of David. In the telling of the story we can see the First Coming of Christ and His return. When Jesus came the first time, He came to give us something to sing about. He came to provide eternal salvation for the souls of men. Yes, Jesus came that first time 2,000 years ago to become a maker of music. He has returned to His Father's house to become a keeper of sheep, but will come again one day — at Armageddon — when the greatest Goliath of history will be amassed against the Jew:

"And David left his carriage in the hand of the keeper of the carriage, and ran into the army, and came and saluted his brethren.

"And as he talked with them, behold, there came up the champion, the Philistine of Gath, Goliath by name, out of the armies of the Philistines, and spake according to the same words: and David heard them.

"And all the men of Israel, when they saw the man, fled from him, and were sore afraid" (I Samuel 17:22-24).

When David came to the battle, he noticed that his comrades were fearful. In like manner, the Battle of Armageddon will find Israel's army so out numbered and overwhelmed that its forces will despair of victory. That giant represents the biggest and most brutal of all battles. According to Revelation 9:16, the number of troops could exceed 200 million — more than any other war in history. Armageddon will be the Goliath of all wars. Every nation in the world will converge its armies upon Israel with one aim — the annihilation of the Jews — an attempt at genocide. It appears that Israel has only one ally today, the United States. However, in that day no nation will come to their aid. Israel will have to stand alone.

David Fights Goliath

David volunteers to fight Goliath. In like manner, at the height of Armageddon, when it looks as if there is no hope for the nation, the scion of David will come to the battle. Sent by His Father, Christ will volunteer to fight the giant and win the day. In this story, one can feel the ill will that has fouled Israel's relationship with her Messiah for twenty centuries:

"And Eliab his eldest brother heard when he spake unto the men; and Eliab's anger was kindled against David, and he said, Why camest thou down hither? and with whom hast thou left those few sheep in the wilderness? I know thy pride, and the naughtiness of thine heart; for thou art come down that thou mightest see the battle.

"And David said, What have I now done? Is there not a cause?

"And he turned from him toward another, and spake after the same manner: and the people answered him again after the former manner" (I Samuel 17:28-30).

Rejected! That has been the case down through history. With all of the good that has come from Christianity, one would think Israel would finally be convinced of His greatness. Christ has impacted civilization more than any other man. Still, He is rejected by His own people. It will take the victory at Armageddon to convince them.

Goliath demands a man — not a committee. The nation needs a man — not a committee. David, confident of his credentials, volunteers to be that man:

"And when the words were heard which David spake, they rehearsed them before Saul: and he sent for him.

"And David said to Saul, Let no man's heart fail because of him; thy servant will go and fight with this Philistine.

"And Saul said to David, Thou art not able to go against this Philistine to fight with him: for thou art but a youth, and he a man of war from his youth" (I Samuel 17:31-33).

No experience! Too young! Those were the sentiments of the king, his troops, and David's brothers. David's youth is typical of Israel on today's battlefields. One must admit that Israel is among the smallest nations in the world, having less than 4 million population, and fields the smallest army. Yet, the Israeli Defense Forces have proven themselves among the most formidable of earth's military might. In the past five decades, Israel has fought numerous battles. Without exception, the IDF has proven to be superior to its enemies.

In spite of its military genius, Israel has another quality shown in David — a willingness to negotiate peace. One can discern from David's writings that he had compassion for those who fought against him. This is so typical of Israel today — willing to give Egypt a conquered Sinai; willing to give its heartland to the Palestinians; willing to yield the Golan

Heights for peace with Syria. All the nation really wants is to live in peace with its neighbors — a commendable quality.

Since World War II, the world's population of Jews has increased to around 14,400,000. One wonders if there is anything prophetic about that number? Even though it is a multiple of the 144,000, mentioned in Revelation 7, it is still quite insignificant among six billion people in today's world. Israel is a nation too small, with borders impossible to defend against the millions of Arabs that surround it.

However, since World War II, Israel has developed a military expertise envied by the rest of the world — as David explains:

"And David said unto Saul, Thy servant kept his father's sheep, and there came a lion, and a bear, and took a lamb out of the flock:

"And I went out after him, and smote him, and delivered it out of his mouth: and when he arose against me, I caught him by his beard, and smote him, and slew him.

"Thy servant slew both the lion and the bear: and this uncircumcised Philistine shall be as one of them, seeing he hath defied the armies of the living God.

"David said moreover, The LORD that delivered me out of the paw of the lion, and out of the paw of the bear, he will deliver me out of the hand of this Philistine. And Saul said unto David, Go, and the LORD be with thee" (I Samuel 17:34-37).

The king had no confidence in the lad, but David explained that he had faced a lion and killed it. What a perfect prophetic picture of Great Britain! The British had control of Jerusalem from 1917 to 1948, but the Jews mounted guerrilla warfare against them and licked the lion.

Then David explained that he had also encountered a bear and killed it. Both of these creatures were every bit as vicious as a giant could be. The bear! What a prophetic picture of the Battle of Gog and Magog! This future invasion is portrayed through the killing of the bear. This generation has witnessed the attack by the lion, but not the bear. It is important to note, however, that the symbol of Russia is a bear. These events in the life of David appear to be a preview of that which is developing in our generation. Perhaps the next major event on God's calendar will be the Russian invasion of Israel — the infamous Battle of Gog and Magog.

If the lion and bear represent end time wars, then the fight with the giant implies that Armageddon is a different battle from Ezekiel's Gog and Magog. Rabbis have equated the war of Ezekiel 38 and 39 with the final battle of history. Yet, there seems to be a difference between David's fight with the bear and his face-off with Goliath. If so, then two great wars lie ahead — seven years apart. Perhaps, Ezekiel 38 opens the Tribulation Period with the Russian invasion and chapter 39 closes it with a final battle.

In the Battle of Armageddon, even the military genius of the IDF will be overwhelmed. Perhaps the following part of David's story will help to explain:

"And Saul armed David with his armour, and he put an helmet of brass upon his head; also he armed him with a coat of mail.

"And David girded his sword upon his armour, and he assayed to go; for he had not proved it. And David said unto Saul, I cannot go with these; for I have not proved them. And David put them off him.

"And he took his staff in his hand, and chose him five smooth stones out of the brook, and put them in a shepherd's bag which he had, even in a scrip; and his sling was in his hand: and he drew near to the Philistine" (I Samuel 17:38-40).

David could not fight with Saul's equipment. Furthermore, he could not afford to be encumbered with it. He needed only his staff and sling. In like manner, Christ will fight the final battle alone. Isaiah writes:

"I have trodden the winepress alone; and of the people there was none with me: for I will tread them in mine anger, and trample them in my fury; and their blood shall be sprinkled upon my garments, and I will stain all my raiment.

"For the day of vengeance is in mine heart, and the year of my redeemed is come.

"And I looked, and there was none to help; and I wondered that there was none to uphold: therefore mine own arm brought salvation unto me; and my fury, it upheld me.

"And I will tread down the people in mine anger, and make them drunk in my fury, and I will bring down their strength to the earth" (Isaiah 63:3-6).

Revelation 19 describes a heavenly host who returns with Christ, but it is Christ who does the fighting:

"And the armies which were in heaven followed him upon white horses, clothed in fine linen, white and clean.

"And out of his mouth goeth a sharp sword, that with it he

should smite the nations: and he shall rule them with a rod of
iron: and he treadeth the winepress of the fierceness and wrath
of Almighty God" (Revelation 19:14,15).

God has a man! David alone runs to meet the giant. Notice that David picks up five smooth stones.
He will only need one to slay Goliath. However, the
giant has four brothers. David prepares a contingency
plan. Thus prepared, he faces the giant:

*"And the Philistine came on and drew near unto David;
and the man that bare the shield went before him.*

*"And when the Philistine looked about, and saw David, he
disdained him: for he was but a youth, and ruddy, and of a
fair countenance.*

*"And the Philistine said unto David, Am I a dog, that thou
comest to me with staves? And the Philistine cursed David by
his gods.*

*"And the Philistine said to David, Come to me, and I will give
thy flesh unto the fowls of the air, and to the beasts of the field.*

*"Then said David to the Philistine, Thou comest to me with
a sword, and with a spear, and with a shield: but I come to
thee in the name of the LORD of hosts, the God of the armies
of Israel, whom thou hast defied.*

*"This day will the LORD deliver thee into mine hand; and
I will smite thee, and take thine head from thee; and I will
give the carcases of the host of the Philistines this day unto
the fowls of the air, and to the wild beasts of the earth; that
all the earth may know that there is a God in Israel.*

*"And all this assembly shall know that the LORD saveth
not with sword and spear: for the battle is the LORD's, and
he will give you into our hands"* (I Samuel 17:41-47).

The battle is the Lord's. He alone will win the final
victory. There is something important in the conver-
sation between David and Goliath. The defeated foe

will be fed to the birds! What more can be said to convince us that Armageddon is the prophetic battle in view here. Revelation 19 describes it:

"And I saw an angel standing in the sun; and he cried with a loud voice, saying to all the fowls that fly in the midst of heaven, Come and gather yourselves together unto the supper of the great God;

"That ye may eat the flesh of kings, and the flesh of captains, and the flesh of mighty men, and the flesh of horses, and of them that sit on them, and the flesh of all men, both free and bond, both small and great" (Revelation 19:17,18).

Ezekiel also mentions a feast by birds:

"And, thou son of man, thus saith the Lord GOD; Speak unto every feathered fowl, and to every beast of the field, Assemble yourselves, and come; gather yourselves on every side to my sacrifice that I do sacrifice for you, even a great sacrifice upon the mountains of Israel, that ye may eat flesh, and drink blood.

"Ye shall eat the flesh of the mighty, and drink the blood of the princes of the earth, of rams, of lambs, and of goats, of bullocks, all of them fatlings of Bashan.

"And ye shall eat fat till ye be full, and drink blood till ye be drunken, of my sacrifice which I have sacrificed for you.

"Thus ye shall be filled at my table with horses and chariots, with mighty men, and with all men of war, saith the Lord GOD" (Ezekiel 39:17-20).

David's Triumphant Victory

David's faith in God is more evident here than perhaps at any other time in his life. Armed with nothing more than a sling, David runs to meet the giant:

"And it came to pass, when the Philistine arose, and came and drew nigh to meet David, that David hasted, and ran toward the army to meet the Philistine.

"And David put his hand in his bag, and took thence a stone, and slang it, and smote the Philistine in his forehead, that the stone sunk into his forehead; and he fell upon his face to the earth.

"So David prevailed over the Philistine with a sling and with a stone, and smote the Philistine, and slew him; but there was no sword in the hand of David" (I Samuel 17:48-50).

To the amazement of his brothers, David makes quick work of the giant. What no other man was willing to attempt, David does! He alone kills the giant and sets the entire Philistine army in disarray:

"Therefore David ran, and stood upon the Philistine, and took his sword, and drew it out of the sheath thereof, and slew him, and cut off his head therewith. And when the Philistines saw their champion was dead, they fled.

"And the men of Israel and of Judah arose, and shouted, and pursued the Philistines, until thou come to the valley, and to the gates of Ekron. And the wounded of the Philistines fell down by the way to Shaaraim, even unto Gath, and unto Ekron" (I Samuel 17:51,52).

The prophetic implications of this story are apparent. Israel is expecting the greater David — Messiah. Though they are trying to negotiate peace with their neighbors, peace continues to be elusive. The Palestinians have no regard for Jewish law or leaders. Also, the Jews have no respect for Yasser Arafat or his 80,000 Palestinian policemen. They cannot trust the Palestinian. They will only have peace when the Messiah appears to insure true peace.

News out of the Middle East, almost daily, tells of military build-up and political unrest. Israel has come to the brink of war several times within the past year. It is only a matter of time until the powder keg in the Middle East explodes into what could become a nuclear war. When the smoke clears away Israel will be victorious.

Israel has yet to kill the bear. That still lies in the future. However, even a victory over Russia, Iran and their allies will not bring the Messiah. It is quite possible that a false messiah will step forward to fool the people into thinking utopia has arrived. Only the Scion of David can win the final victory and set up a Kingdom that will last a thousand years. That Messiah is Jesus Christ.

Chapter Fifteen

The Wisdom of Solomon

Solomon's life was orchestrated by the heavenly Father to offer a prophetic story of the promised messiah. The heritage he represented; the wisdom he displayed; the kingdom he ruled; the temple he built; even the wives he married find their prophetic fulfillment in the life and ministry of Christ.

Solomon was the wisest man of his day, but in Matthew 12:42, our Savior said, *"... a greater than Solomon is here,"* David may have had Solomon in mind when he penned the second Psalm, but prophetically, he envisioned the future *"Son"* who would sit upon his throne: *"Thou art my Son; this day have I begotten thee" (Psalm 2:7).*

This verse was quoted by the Apostle Paul in Acts 13:33. Referring to his Jewish ancestors, he wrote:

"God hath fulfilled the same unto us their children, in that he hath raised up Jesus again; as it is also written in the second psalm, Thou art my Son, this day have I begotten thee." (Acts 13:33)

The verse sets forth a double reference, first to Solomon and then to Christ, making Solomon a prophetic type of the Savior.

The Birth of Solomon

The first son of David and Bathsheba died at the age of seven days, but God forgave that scarlet sin and gave them another child — Solomon:

"... she bare a son, and he called his name Solomon: and the LORD loved him.
"And he sent by the hand of Nathan the prophet; and he called his name Jedidiah, because of the LORD" (II Samuel 12:24,25).

Jedidiah means "beloved of the Lord." It reminds us of the day God said: *"This is my beloved son, in whom I am well pleased"* (Matthew 3:17). Jesus Christ was the greater Jedidiah. He was beloved of the Lord. The name Solomon, meaning "peace," is also indicative of Christ, the Prince of Peace.

Solomon was the second son of David and Bathsheba. The death of the first son seems indicative of Adam who, though he was the first federal head of the human race, died as a result of sin. Solomon reminds us of the second Adam, Jesus Christ, who came to replace and redeem the one who was lost. In a symbolic way, Solomon took the place of Bathsheba's first son, just as Christ took the place of Adam.

The Symbolic David

We are told that David was a man after God's own heart. He represents a wealth of prophetic truth. Zechariah, writing about the future battle over Jerusalem, likens the house of David to God, Himself:

"In that day shall the LORD defend the inhabitants of Jerusalem; and he that is feeble among them at that day shall be as David; and the house of David shall be as God, as the angel of the LORD before them" (Zechariah 12:8).

The kingship of David is symbolic of God who is King of the universe. When David fathered a baby who died and a second son who sat upon his throne, he reveals a prophetic view of God whose first Adam died and whose second Adam will rule this world as King of kings. Furthermore, the house of David eventually produced the Son of God, fulfilling the prophecy that *"the house of David shall be as God."*

Before Solomon, however, there was another pretender to the throne. Absalom tried to overthrow David's authority, just as Lucifer is trying to usurp the throne of God. In fact, the devil will continue his evil quest until he is finally thrown into the lake of fire. Absalom becomes a type of Lucifer.

Solomon Becomes King

When David was old and sick, Abishag, a young and beautiful Shunammite virgin was chosen to be his nurse and keep him warm. Knowing that David would soon die, Adonijah, the brother of Absalom, conspired with Joab, captain of the military, and Abiathar, the high priest, to declare himself as the next king. He threw a feast to celebrate his ascent to David's throne, but Nathan informed Bathsheba and urged her to report the sedition to David.

Bathsheba went to the ailing king and reminded him of the promise that Solomon would be the next king. David agreed and gave instructions to take Solomon to the Gihon Spring and anoint him as Israel's new king. The whole city of Jerusalem rejoiced at David's decision. The noise of the cheering crowd could be heard throughout the city as they celebrated the coronation of their new king.

A messenger hurried to Adonijah's party with the news that Solomon had been crowned. Fearing the new king, the party broke up and Adonijah went to Gibeon — to the Mosaic tabernacle for safety. This reminds me of the Antichrist who will commit the abomination of desolation in an attempt to establish his own world kingdom:

"And it was told Solomon, saying, Behold, Adonijah feareth king Solomon: for, lo, he hath caught hold on the horns of the altar, saying, Let king Solomon swear unto me to day that he will not slay his servant with the sword.

"And Solomon said, If he will show himself a worthy man, there shall not an hair of him fall to the earth: but if wickedness shall be found in him, he shall die.

"So king Solomon sent, and they brought him down from the altar. And he came and bowed himself to king Solomon: and Solomon said unto him, Go to thine house" (I Kings 1:51-53).

Solomon gave Adonijah the opportunity to live in peace. It was not the nature of the new king to hold a grudge. However, Solomon did not expect what happened next. Adonijah went to Bathsheba and asked her to request that Solomon give him Abishag for his wife — the young virgin whose body had kept David warm! This reminds me of the true purpose of the Antichrist, son of the serpent. He wants the virgin who was chosen for God, namely, the Church, the bride of Christ:

"And king Solomon answered and said unto his mother, And why dost thou ask Abishag the Shunammite for Adonijah? ask for him the kingdom also" (I Kings 2:22).

In Solomon's thinking, this was tantamount to asking for the throne, itself.

What happened next is indicative of the judgment of the wicked at the return of Christ. Adonijah was executed for trying to take over the kingdom, typical of the fate of the Antichrist.

Next, Joab, head of the military, was executed for shedding innocent blood — a prophetic scenario of the soldiers who will be slain at the Battle of Armageddon. Then, Abiathar, offspring of Eli, was removed from the office of high priest and replaced with Zadok. This offers a prophetic scenario of the replacement of the Levitical priesthood with the Melchizedek priesthood at the return of Christ.

The Judgment of Shimei

Then there was the judgment of Shimei. This Benjamite of the house of Saul was bitter over the fact that David ascended the throne upon the death of Israel's wicked king. When David left Jerusalem during Absalom's attempt to overthrow the kingdom, Shimei threw rocks at David and cursed him. He accused him of taking the kingdom from Saul:

"And thus said Shimei when he cursed, Come out, come out, thou bloody man, and thou man of Belial:
"The LORD hath returned upon thee all the blood of the house of Saul, in whose stead thou hast reigned; and the LORD hath delivered the kingdom into the hand of Absalom thy son: and, behold, thou art taken in thy mischief, because thou art a bloody man" (II Samuel 16:7,8).

David let him get away with it at the time, but Solomon was instructed to bring judgment upon him. It reminds us of the judgment of the nations because of their ill treatment of the Chosen People. Solomon put Shimei under house arrest in Jerusalem and forbade him from leaving Jerusalem under threat of death. In like manner, Christ will judge the nations and rule them with a rod of iron.

Solomon married Pharaoh's daughter. In Scripture, Egypt is a type of the world. Therefore, this reminds us of the bride of Christ who will be chosen from the world. In fact, Solomon's marriage to many Gentiles (700 wives and 300 concubines) indicates that the Church will be made up of a great host of believers from all nations.

Solomon's First Encounter with God

Solomon went to the tabernacle at Gibeon, the place where both Adonijah and Joab had taken hold of the horns of the altar. It was also the place where Joshua had made the sun stand still. Solomon's journey reminds us of Christ who will come to the scene of the world's last great epic battle — Armageddon.

At Gibeon, Solomon offered a thousand burnt offerings upon the altar. They may be typical of the millennial reign of Christ — the rule of a thousand years. That night, the Lord appeared to Solomon in a dream. It was the first of three special contacts, in which God was to speak to him:

"In Gibeon, the LORD appeared to Solomon in a dream by night: and God said, Ask what I shall give thee" (I Kings 3:5).

Rather than asking for riches or peace from his enemies, Solomon asked for wisdom:

"Give therefore thy servant an understanding heart to judge thy people, that I may discern between good and bad: for who is able to judge this thy so great a people?" (I Kings 3:9).

The request pleased the Lord. Solomon was given a keenness of mind and a mental quality which surpassed the other kings of his day. Also, God gave him both riches and honor — those things for which he had not asked.

"Behold, I have done according to thy words: lo, I have given thee a wise and an understanding heart; so that there was none like thee before thee, neither after thee shall any arise like unto thee.

"And I have also given thee that which thou hast not asked, both riches, and honor: so that there shall not be any among the kings like unto thee all thy days" (I Kings 3:12,13).

In like manner, when Jesus came the first time, He did not yield to the temptation to sit upon the throne of this world. He declined the opportunity of great riches and the conquest of the Romans. Instead of sitting upon a throne, He chose to hang upon a cross and called that His *"hour of glory."* To the average person, it may not have seemed to be a wise choice. It has since become obvious that Christ exhibited the greater wisdom — for in His death, He provided eternal life for us. Because Christ declined both the riches of this world and the conquest of His enemies, He shall be given both some day. He will come to the defense of Israel in the height of the Battle of Armageddon. At that time, He shall obtain the destruction of His enemies and establish His Kingdom's golden age of peace and prosperity.

Solomon's Second Encounter

Solomon's second encounter with God came at the completion of the temple:

"And the LORD said unto him, I have heard thy prayer and thy supplication, that thou hast made before me: I have hallowed this house, which thou hast built, to put my name there for ever; and mine eyes and mine heart shall be there perpetually.

"And if thou wilt walk before me, as David thy father walked, in integrity of heart, and in uprightness, to do according to all that I have commanded thee, and wilt keep my statues and my judgments:

"Then I will establish the throne of thy kingdom upon Israel for ever, as I promised to David thy father, saying, There shall not fail thee a man upon the throne of Israel" (I Kings 9:3-5).

This promise of perpetuity had certain conditions attached to it. God warned Solomon that if he failed to keep his commandments, Israel would be cut off:

"But if ye shall at all turn from following me, ye or your children, and will not keep my commandments and my statutes which I have set before you, but go and serve other gods, and worship them:

"Then will I cut off Israel out of the land which I have given them; and this house, which I have hallowed for my name, will I cast out of my sight; and Israel shall be a proverb and a byword among all people" (I Kings 9:6,7).

Unfortunately, Solomon did not keep his word. He failed to be the perfect example of the future Messiah. He allowed his heart to be turned away from the worship of God.

Solomon's Third Encounter

God made one more appearance before Solomon — and His verdict was devastating:

"Wherefore the LORD said unto Solomon, Forasmuch as this is done of thee, and thou hast not kept my covenant and my statutes, which I have commanded thee, I will surely rend the kingdom from thee, and will give it to thy servant" (I Kings 11:11).

During his reign, Solomon married the daughter of Pharaoh, women of the Moabites, Ammonites, Edomites, and other nations around Israel. As earlier noted, he had 700 wives and 300 concubines. As Solomon grew old, his wives turned away his heart to serve other gods. For this, God divided his kingdom and gave the northern ten tribes to his servant, Jeroboam.

It is sad that even though Solomon represented a prophetic type of the Savior, he was still, at best, an imperfect representation of the future perfect King. Like those before him, Solomon failed the test.

Adam failed the test in the Garden of Eden. Noah failed after the Flood when he drank the wine. Abraham failed when he produced a child by Hagar instead of waiting upon the promise of God. Moses failed when he smote the rock the second time instead of speaking to it. In every case, though these great men were prophetic types of Jesus Christ, they were plagued by human imperfections.

Builder of the Temple

The first program established by King Solomon was the building of a magnificent temple to the glory of God. Until then, God had resided in a tent. His father, David, was only allowed to gather the materials for its construction:

"Whereas I have not dwelt in any house since the time that I brought up the children of Israel out of Egypt, even to this day, but have walked in a tent and in a tabernacle.

" In all the places wherein I have walked with all the children of Israel spake I a word with any of the tribes of Israel, whom I commanded to feed my people Israel, saying, Why build ye not me an house of cedar?" (II Samuel 7:6,7).

David desired to build the temple, but God refused, saying that he had been a man of war and was not qualified to build the temple. Instead, God gave the privilege to Solomon:

"But the word of the LORD came to me, saying, Thou hast shed blood abundantly, and hast made great wars: thou shalt not build an house unto my name, because thou hast shed much blood upon the earth in my sight.

"Behold, a son shall be born to thee, who shall be a man of rest; and I will give him rest from all his enemies round about: for his name shall be Solomon, and I will give peace and quietness unto Israel in his days.

"He shall build an house for my name; and he shall be my son, and I will be his father; and I will establish the throne of his kingdom over Israel forever." (I Chronicles 22:8-10).

Solomon's temple was regarded as one of the masterpieces of ancient architecture. It stood for four hundred years. Potentates from many nations came to observe the greatness of Solomon. It is said that silver was as plentiful as stones in Jerusalem. His reign was a marvel to the world.

As one greater than Solomon, our Savior will build the third temple. Haggai promised that the final temple would surpass the glory of Solomon:

"The glory of this latter house shall be greater than of the former, saith the LORD of hosts: and in this place will I give peace, saith the LORD of hosts" (Haggai 2:9).

Until that wonderful day, may we be reminded that Christ has allowed all who believe in Him to become the building blocks of a spiritual temple. Our bodies are the dwelling place of the Holy Spirit.

Jesus told the Samaritan woman in John, chapter 4, that there would come a day when men would no longer worship God at the Samaritan temple built on Mt. Gerizim, or even in the temple at Jerusalem, but that men would worship God in spirit and in truth. We have become the fulfillment of His prophecy. We are the temple of God.

On the Day of Pentecost, the Holy Spirit descended from heaven and sat upon the believers, filling them with God's presence. The Apostle Paul later explained:

"What? know ye not that your body is the temple of the Holy Ghost which is in you, which ye have of God, and ye are not your own?
"For ye are bought with a price: therefore glorify God in your body, and in your spirit, which are God's." (I Corinthians 6:19,20).

When John saw the holy city, New Jerusalem, he remarked that there was no temple in it. We are the epitome of that temple. On a more physical plane, however, when Christ returns, He will build a magnificent third temple on Mt. Moriah at the site of Solomon's first edifice. Zechariah wrote:

"Even he shall build the temple of the LORD; and he shall bear the glory, and shall sit and rule upon his throne." (Zechariah 6:13).

Some years ago, I discussed Jewish plans for a third temple with an archeologist in Jerusalem. He was in charge of the excavation along the western wall of the temple site. I asked if he was excavating the area in order to prepare for the building of a Jewish temple. He replied that he had no personal plans to build such a temple, but that a temple would be built one day by the Messiah when He comes.

He said that a temple could not be built at this time because of the continuing wars between the Arabs and the Jews. He said that the Jewish people were not going to build a temple, only to have it destroyed again. He made it clear that when there is lasting peace in the world and the Messiah has come, then a third temple will be built.

The Books of Solomon

Three main aspects of Solomon's life are reflected in the books he wrote. First, as the builder of the temple, Solomon compiled the Proverbs. They represent instructions for the building of our lives — for we have become the temple of God. Secondly, as a demonstration of his earthly wisdom, Solomon wrote the book of Ecclesiastes.

Thirdly, as one who took a Gentile bride, Solomon wrote the Song of Solomon. These three books present three major areas of his reign. They present a prophetic view of Christ who is the ultimate fulfillment of Solomon.

It took Solomon twenty years to build his palace and the temple. I do not know if that represents a prophecy in times, but it is interesting to note that Christ has spent the last twenty centuries in another building program — one in which we are called *"lively stones"* (I Pet. 2:5). Could that mean that His building program is about to be completed and the last stone put in place?

It is also interesting to note that Solomon took the throne of Israel around a thousand years B.C. One thousand years later, Christ was born. Though Solomon did not reign all of this time, it does seem to remind us of the 1,000 year reign of Christ.

While on the subject of times, may we take note that Saul, David, and Solomon each reigned forty years. The tenure of these men may be a prophetic overview of the past 6,000 years of human history — with each year representing a corresponding jubilee.

The reign of Saul, being forty years duration, seems to correspond with the first 2,000 years of human history. Two thousand years lapsed between Adam and Abraham — the time it would take for forty jubilees. The reign of David, being forty years duration, seems to be typical of the next 2,000 years of human history — from Abraham to Christ. Finally, the reign of Solomon seems to be a prophetic overview of these past 2000 years.

Three Major Prophecies

When our Savior comes He will fulfill three major prophecies presented in the life of Solomon. First He will build the third and final temple. Secondly, He will exhibit great wisdom as Judge of all the earth. Thirdly, He will take unto Himself those multiplied millions who make up the bride of Christ. We now await the return of Christ, our blessed hope. We are waiting for the shout and trumpet sound. May He come in our day.

Chapter Sixteen

The Promise of Elijah

Elijah is one of the most beloved men in the Old Testament. His life offers a shining example of steadfastness and courage, having remained faithful in the midst of national apostasy. As a result of his outstanding ministry, Elijah was translated — taken alive into heaven, engendering a promise that someday he would return to introduce the Messiah. Malachi, the last of the writing prophets, expressed this blessed hope with a direct word from God:

"Behold, I will send you Elijah the prophet before the coming of the great and dreadful day of the LORD:
"And he shall turn the heart of the fathers to the children, and the heart of the children to their fathers, lest I come and smite the earth with a curse" (Malachi 4:5,6).

According to Malachi, Elijah should come just prior to the *"... great and dreadful day of the LORD."*

Though early prophets did not fully understand just when that day would occur, they generally followed the concept laid out by Moses that the seven days of Creation represented seven thousand years in mankind's great adventure. The seventh millennium should correspond to the seventh day wherein God rested from His creative work. For that reason, hope is alive that Elijah will soon appear.

Down through the centuries, the promise of Elijah's return has kept the flame of hope alive in the Jewish heart. In the midst of national tragedies, the children of Israel have pressed on in the hope that the great prophet will appear on some future Passover to announce the Advent of the Messiah.

As the fifth millennium commenced, religious Jews were looking for the Messiah. Typically speaking, the fourth millennium, corresponding to Wednesday of the Creation week, was coming to a close and Thursday was dawning. Since virgins were wed on Wednesdays and previously married women were usually remarried on Thursdays, there was good reason to expect the Messiah to appear. After all, they considered Israel as the wife of Jehovah awaiting reconciliation. With messianic expectations running high, it is perplexing that the religious hierarchy did not accept Jesus' credentials. Nor did they recognize the new Elijah — John the Baptist.

The Mount of Transfiguration

After the death of John, Elijah appeared with Moses and Jesus on the Mount of Transfiguration. His brief visit offered a further prophetic foreview of the future day of the Lord:

"And after six days Jesus taketh Peter, James, and John his brother, and bringeth them up into an high mountain apart,

"And was transfigured before them: and his face did shine as the sun, and his raiment was white as the light.

"And, behold, there appeared unto them Moses and Elias [Elijah] talking with him" (Matthew 17:1-3).

Elijah came back that day, but not to stay. His appearance was only a brief reminder that the Chosen People must continue to wait patiently for the Messianic Kingdom. Jesus asked His three closest disciples to keep quiet about Elijah's visit:

"And as they came down from the mountain, Jesus charged them, saying, Tell the vision to no man, until the Son of man be risen again from the dead.

"And his disciples asked him, saying, Why then say the scribes that Elias must first come?" (Matthew 17:9,10).

Peter, James and John were familiar with the long-held view that Elijah should return, but expressed their confusion over his all-too-brief visit. It was here that they were reminded of a profound truth. At least part of Malachi's prophecy was fulfilled in the person of John the Baptist:

*"And Jesus answered and said unto them, Elias truly shall
first come, and restore all things.*

*"But I say unto you, That Elias is come already, and they
knew him not, but have done unto him whatsoever they listed.
Likewise shall also the Son of man suffer of them.*

*"Then the disciples understood that he spake unto them of
John the Baptist"* (Matthew 17:11-13).

Earlier, the Savior had referred to John as being a
prophetic fulfillment of the promised Elijah:

"For all the prophets and the law prophesied until John.

*"And if you will receive it, this is Elijah which was for to
come"* (Matthew 11:13,14).

John the Baptist

Whether John fulfilled the prophecy is not a matter of debate. Gabriel made this clear when he met
John's father and announced that the child would
grow up in the spirit and power of Elijah:

*"But the angel said unto him, Fear not, Zacharias: for thy
prayer is heard; and thy wife Elisabeth shall bear thee a son,
and thou shalt call his name John.*

*"And thou shalt have joy and gladness; and many shall
rejoice at his birth.*

*"For he shall be great in the sight of the Lord, and shall
drink neither wine nor strong drink; and he shall be filled
with the Holy Ghost, even from his mother's womb.*

*"And many of the children of Israel shall he turn to the
Lord their God.*

"And he shall go before him in the spirit and power of Elias
[Elijah], *to turn the hearts of the fathers to the children, and
the disobedient to the wisdom of the just; to make ready a
people prepared for the Lord"* (Luke 1:13-17).

Just how God accomplished this return of Elijah is not clear. We are told that when Mary came to visit Elizabeth, the yet unborn baby leaped for joy:

"And it came to pass, that, when Elisabeth heard the salutation of Mary, the babe leaped in her womb; and Elisabeth was filled with the Holy Ghost" (Luke 1:41).

Only divine terms could explain how the unborn infant knew what was going on. John was filled with the Holy Spirit before birth — a seeming impossibility. Luke, an accredited physician, accepted the fact and had no reservations about it. John was no ordinary human being. He was the returned Elijah.

Reincarnation?

Christian theologians (myself among them) stand opposed to the concept of reincarnation. This heretical teaching was spawned by Eastern mysticism and is a major tenet of Buddhism and Hinduism. It is absurd to think that one could return as another human being on some mystical journey to fulfill their karma.

However, the Bible does teach that we can be visited, even possessed by other spirits — either evil or holy. Essentially, we are spirits who live in and control our physical bodies — with the ability to invite other spirits to enter. Jesus cast evil spirits out of people. Though not every mental problem can be attributed to an evil spirit, some, no doubt, can.

Shortly after their encounter with Moses and Elijah, Jesus, Peter, James and John rejoined the others at the foot of the hill. Jesus found the disciples trying to cast an evil spirit out of a child. The father came to the Savior with his poor child and explained that the disciples were unable to cure him:

"And Jesus rebuked the devil; and he departed out of him: and the child was cured from that very hour.

"Then came the disciples to Jesus apart, and said, Why could not we cast him out?

"And Jesus said unto them, Because of your unbelief: for verily I say unto you, If ye have faith as a grain of mustard seed, ye shall say unto this mountain, Remove hence to yonder place; and it shall remove; and nothing shall be impossible unto you.

"Howbeit this kind goeth not out but by prayer and fasting" (Matthew 17:18-21).

The fact that spirits have the ability to enter and control our bodies cannot be denied. It is a biblical concept. Furthermore, at the moment we invite Christ into our hearts, the Holy Spirit regenerates our spirit with eternal life. We are "born again." Though we do not understand the mechanics of such a phenomenon, we must admit that the Bible teaches it. Therefore, we have no alternative but to agree that God, by special dispensation, allowed the spirit of Elijah to visit the spirit of John the Baptist.

Elijah Must Come Twice

According to rabbinical teachings, Malachi's prophecy was to be fulfilled in two phases. It was commonly believed Elijah would come twice — the first time to introduce the Messiah and the second time in the midst of Ezekiel's predicted Battle of Gog and Magog:

"In the second year of the reign of Ahaziah, Elijah became hidden, and was seen no more. When the King Messiah shall come, he will be seen again, then hidden a second time. He will not be seen again until Gog and Magog appear on the scene" (*Seder Olam*).

The final installment of Malachi's prophecy should occur during the future Battle of Gog and Magog. Elijah is predicted to make his appearance on a Passover to prepare Israel for the Messianic Kingdom. Early rabbis expected two messiahs — Messiah ben [son of] Joseph and Messiah ben [son of] David. They taught that a scion of Joseph would die for their sins and that a son of David would win the war against Gog. This is how they accounted for the scriptural teaching that the Messiah would both suffer and reign. They were not aware that the Messiah would come twice, but God knew it and planned for Elijah's return. The promised Elijah came two thousand years ago to announce the First Coming of Christ and will return someday to announce His Second Advent.

The Voice in the Wilderness

Isaiah also addressed the concept that Elijah would return for the purpose of preparing the Chosen People to receive their Messiah. Though he did not name Elijah as the specific prophet, he described the wilderness of Judea as the general area from which he would come:

"Comfort ye, comfort ye my people, saith your God.

"Speak ye comfortably to Jerusalem, and cry unto her, that her warfare is accomplished, that her iniquity is pardoned: for she hath received of the LORD's hand double for all her sins.

"The voice of **him** *that crieth in the wilderness, Prepare ye the way of the LORD, make straight in the desert a highway for our God"* (Isaiah 40:1-3).

John was that *"voice in the wilderness."* We are told that his ministry was located just east of Jericho at the Jordan River — in the wilderness of Judea. This was either at or near the place where Elijah was last seen. We are told that the sons of the prophets had watched Elijah cross the Jordan River:

"And fifty men of the sons of the prophets went, and stood to view afar off: and they two [Elijah and Elisha] *stood by Jordan.*

"And Elijah took his mantle, and wrapped it together, and smote the waters, and they were divided hither and thither, so that they two went over on dry ground" (II Kings 2:7,8).

The pair ascended Mount Nebo. Only Elisha returned. A search made for Elijah proved fruitless.

Elijah had boarded a celestial vehicle which had landed on the summit to transport him into heaven. Elisha had witnessed his translation:

"And it came to pass, as they still went on, and talked, that, behold, there appeared a chariot of fire, and horses of fire, and parted them both asunder; and Elijah went up by a whirlwind into heaven.

"And Elisha saw it, and he cried, My father, my father, the chariot of Israel, and the horsemen thereof. And he saw him no more: and he took hold of his own clothes, and rent them in two pieces.

"He took up also the mantle of Elijah that fell from him, and went back, and stood by the bank of Jordan;

"And he took the mantle of Elijah that fell from him, and smote the waters, and said, Where is the LORD God of Elijah? and when he also had smitten the waters, they parted hither and thither: and Elisha went over" (II Kings 2:11-14).

Elisha's question dealt with whether God had endued him with a double portion of Elijah's power — *"Where is the LORD God of Elijah?"* However, the sons of the prophets were wondering where is the Elijah of God? They embarked upon a search, but were unable to find him.

In the course of time, the great prophet returned to the Jordan River in the form of John the Baptist and partially carried out the ministry foretold by Malachi. Someday, just as the rabbis teach, Elijah will return again to complete his divine mission.

Elijah and John

There are several comparisons between Elijah and John the Baptist. For example, Elijah dwelt by the brook Cherith, a tributary that emptied into the Jordan River. In like manner, John the Baptist lived by the Jordan River. Elijah had a strange diet. He was fed by the ravens. Similarly, John had a strange diet of locusts and wild honey.

King Ahaziah's soldiers described Elijah as "hairy." Rabbis say that he was wearing a "hairy" tallit — made of camel's hair and a priestly leather girdle:

"And they answered him, He was an hairy man, and girt with a girdle of leather about his loins. And he said, It is Elijah the Tishbite" (II Kings 1:8).

In like manner, John wore a *"... raiment of camel's hair, and a leathern girdle about his loins"* (Matthew 3:4). It is possible that he wore Elijah's mantle and priestly leather girdle. These items were kept near the Golden Altar of Incense — the very place where Zecharias had his encounter with Gabriel.

Perhaps Elijah's mantle and girdle were handed over to Zecharias by none other than Gabriel himself! The strange attire must have signaled the religious leaders at the Temple in Jerusalem that Elijah had arrived.

Elijah denounced Israel's King Ahab for his sins. Like the prophet before him, John also denounced King Herod for his sins, thus leading to John's arrest and execution. There was a human side to Elijah. He fled from the threat of Jezebel. In like manner, there was a similar human frailty observed in John who, while in prison, doubted his calling and sent a message to Jesus asking if He really was the Messiah.

Elijah and Elisha Compared

These and other comparisons are typical of both Elijah and John. However, Elijah performed several recorded miracles, while John performed none. It seems odd that John, having the power of Elijah, would not demonstrate that divine ability. However, John's lack of miracles may be due to Elisha, who asked Elijah for a double portion of his spirit:

"And it came to pass, when they were gone over, that Elijah said unto Elisha, Ask what I shall do for thee, before I be taken away from thee. And Elisha said, I pray thee, let a double portion of thy spirit be upon me.

"And he said, Thou hast asked a hard thing: nevertheless, if thou see me when I am taken from thee, it shall be so unto thee; but if not, it shall not be so" (II Kings 2:9,10).

Elisha received Elijah's power that day and went on to perform exactly twice as many miracles. Therefore, John may have been limited — not in power, but in the fulfillment of Elijah's promise to Elisha.

Elijah's Miracles

1. He caused a drought that lasted three and a half years (I Kings 17:1).
2. He provided food for a widow and her son (I Kings 17:16).
3. He raised a twelve year old boy from the dead (I Kings 17:22).
4. He called fire down from heaven on Mount Carmel (I Kings 18:36-38).
5. He called down fire upon the soldiers who would capture him (II Kings 1:10).
6. He called fire down upon a second group of soldiers (II Kings 1:12).
7. He parted the waters of the Jordan River (II Kings 2:8).

Elisha's Miracles

1. He also parted the waters of the Jordan with Elijah's mantle (II Kings 2:14).
2. He healed the bitter waters of Jericho (II Kings 2:19).
3. He cursed the mocking children and two bears devoured them (II Kings 2:24).
4. He multiplied a pot of oil for the widow and her sons (II Kings 4:1).
5. He promised a son to the Shunammite woman (II Kings 4:16).
6. He raised the Shunammite woman's child from the dead (II Kings 4:35).
7. He cured the poisonous pot of pottage (II Kings 4:41).
8. He healed Naaman of leprosy (II Kings 5:10).
9. He cursed Gehazi with Naaman's leprosy (II Kings 5:27).
10. He made an iron axe head float on water (II Kings 6:6).
11. He opened the eyes of his servant to see God's army surrounding Dothan and caused his captors to be blinded (II Kings 6:17,18).

12. Elisha predicted the deliverance of Samaria from the Syrians (II Kings 6:16,17).

13. He predicted the death of Benhadad at the hands of Hazael (II Kings 8:13).

14. After Elisha's death, a soldier was revived when his body was tossed upon the prophet's bones — thus making exactly twice as many miracles as was recorded of Elijah (II Kings 13:21).

Elisha demonstrated a double portion of Elijah's power. Perhaps for that reason, John was limited. However, when Elijah returns as one of the two witnesses during the Tribulation period, he will again demonstrate his power to cause a drought and call fire down upon his enemies:

"And I will give power unto my two witnesses, and they shall prophesy a thousand two hundred and threescore days, clothed in sackcloth.

"These are the two olive trees, and the two candlesticks standing before the God of the earth.

"And if any man will hurt them, fire proceedeth out of their mouth, and devoureth their enemies: and if any man will hurt them, he must in this manner be killed.

"These have power to shut heaven, that it rain not in the days of their prophecy: and have power over waters to turn them to blood, and to smite the earth with all plagues, as often as they will" (Revelation 11:3-6).

Why the future Elijah will perform miracles when John the Baptist did not is perplexing. However, we should note that two of the miracles recounted are the same as those performed by Elijah — calling upon fire to devour their enemies and shutting up heaven to cause a drought.

Elijah and Moses

The two witnesses will demonstrate miracles that marked the ministries of Elijah and Moses, the same two men who met with Jesus on the Mount of Transfiguration. Moses was the man who *"turned water into blood"* and released *"plagues."* The appearance of Israel's lawgiver and renowned prophet displayed a prophetic foreview of the Second Coming of Christ *"in the glory of His Father."* Furthermore, Jesus referred to this occasion as being a prophetic picture of *"the Son of Man coming in His kingdom."*

Obviously, John the Baptist was not the final fulfillment of the prophecy. Elijah is due to have another ministry during the Tribulation. Because of this prediction of a future Elijah, we would do well to go back to the story of Elijah and review those events which surrounded his ministry in order to observe a prophetic pattern of those things which shall occur during the Tribulation Period.

Ahab and Jezebel

Elijah ministered during the reign of Ahab and Jezebel. Ahab appears to be a type of the Antichrist who compromised his Jewish heritage and married the wicked Jezebel — a type of Mystery Babylon. John explains Jezebel's relationship to the Tribulation Period:

"Not withstanding I have a few things against thee, because thou sufferest that woman Jezebel, which calleth herself a prophetess, to teach and to seduce my servants to commit fornication, and to eat things sacrificed unto idols.

"And I gave her space to repent of her fornication; and she repented not.

"Behold, I will cast her into a bed, and them that commit adultery with her into great tribulation ..." (Rev. 2:20-22).

God has promised to cast the prophetic Jezebel, along with all those who consort with her, into *"great tribulation."* This lays out a concept similar to the judgment of Mystery Babylon. We are told that Jezebel introduced Baal worship throughout the northern kingdom — the same religion as Mystery Babylon. It is the old Babylonian system which has continued to oppose the worship of God down through the ages.

Naboth's Vineyard

As the story proceeds, we find that King Ahab coveting the vineyard of Naboth:

"And it came to pass after these things, that Naboth the Jezreelite had a vineyard, which was in Jezreel, hard by the palace of Ahab king of Samaria.

"And Ahab spake unto Naboth, saying, Give me thy vineyard, that I may have it for a garden of herbs, because it is near unto my house: and I will give thee for it a better vineyard than it; or, if it seem good to thee, I will give thee the worth of it in money.

"And Naboth said to Ahab, The LORD forbid it me, that I should give the inheritance of my fathers unto thee" (I Kings 21:1-3).

The vineyard of Naboth prophetically typifies that garden spot of the world — the land of Israel. Though the Antichrist will virtually control the world, he will set his eyes on Jerusalem and desire the holy city for his world capital.

According to the story, Ahab pouted because the righteous Naboth would not give up the inheritance of his fathers. Naboth represents the Chosen People who, after all these centuries, have finally gone back home to the land of their forefathers. The land of Israel today rightly belongs to the Jews.

In the Tribulation Period, the Antichrist will set his sights on Jerusalem and the land of Israel. His goal will be to internationalize the city. When he finds himself unsuccessful, his wife Jezebel (typical of Mystery Babylon) will create a lie against the Jews — blaming them of blasphemy just as the wicked Jezebel stirred up anti-Semitic feelings against the righteous Naboth.

Jezebel wrote a letter to the elders of Jezreel:

"And she wrote in the letters, saying, Proclaim a fast, and set Naboth on high among the people:
"And set two men, sons of Belial, before him, to bear witness against him, saying, Thou didst blaspheme God and the king. And then carry him out, and stone him, that he may die" (I Kings 21:9,10).

The story offers a prophetic scenario similar to what is happening in Israel today. Naboth is being falsely accused all over again. The prophetic Jezebel is determined to take the land from the Jews and give it to the Antichrist. In the midst of the Tribulation, she will succeed. The Antichrist will march into Jerusalem, enter the temple and commit the abomination of desolation. Essentially, that is what Ahab did when he went down to the vineyard of Naboth to take possession of it.

Elijah Meets Ahab

Lurking in the shadows of the vineyard was the prophet Elijah. Ahab was startled:

"Hast thou found me, O mine enemy? And he answered, I have found thee: because thou hast sold thyself to work evil in the sight of the LORD" (I Kings 21:20).

How do we know this represents the abomination of desolation? What causes us to think Jezebel represents Mystery Babylon and that Ahab typifies the Antichrist? Perhaps it is because of Elijah's message given in verse 24:

"Him that dieth of Ahab in the city the dogs shall eat; and him that dieth in the field shall the fowls of the air eat" (I Kings 21:24).

Because of the wickedness of Ahab and Jezebel, Elijah promised that birds will eat the flesh of the slain on the battlefield. This is similar to the description of the Battle of Armageddon:

"And I saw an angel standing in the sun; and he cried with a loud voice, saying to all the fowls that fly in the midst of heaven, Come and gather yourselves together unto the supper of the great God;

"That ye may eat the flesh of kings, and the flesh of cap-tains, and the flesh of mighty men, and the flesh of horses, and of them that sit on them, and the flesh of all men, both free and bond, both small and great" (Revelation 19:17,18). Ahab and Jezebel will find their prophetic fulfillment at Armageddon.

When Ahab married Jezebel, Elijah came forth to declare a drought which lasted three and one-half years. According to Revelation 11, another drought will occur for three and one-half years during the ministry of the prophetic Elijah.

But how could such a thing occur? How could there be a worldwide drought — a lack of rain throughout all the world for a period of three and one-half years? In 1973, *U.S. News and World Report* declared that the world had entered a new era — the era of fam-ine. That year, six million people died of starvation or of some related disease. By 1976 the number of those dying among the starving masses reached 20 million.

In this decade, over 50 million people die of star-vation every year. However, when the Tribulation Period begins, all rain will be halted throughout the world. How could this be? Perhaps the prophetic Battle of Gog and Magog (possibly a worldwide nuclear war) could interrupt world weather patterns. Of course, it does not have to be caused that way. God can do anything.

The Contest of Fire

At the end of three and one-half years of drought, Elijah went to Mt. Carmel to challenge the prophets of Baal. He repaired the altar of the Lord that was broken and called fire down from heaven. He did this in order to turn the hearts of the people back to God. This could be a prophetic picture of what will occur during the Tribulation period. Malachi predicted that the future Elijah will come to *"turn the hearts of the fathers to the children."*

Elijah repaired the altar of the Lord, prepared a sacrifice, and had twelve barrels of water poured upon it. This could be a prophecy of the future erection of David's tabernacle, the cleansing of its sanctuary and the restoration of sacrificial worship.

Jezebel's Threat

After the great event on Mt. Carmel, Jezebel threatened Elijah:

"Then Jezebel sent a messenger unto Elijah, saying, So let the gods do to me, and more also, if I make not thy life as the life on one of them by to morrow about this time.

"And when he saw that, he arose, and went for his life ..." (I Kings 19:2,3).

This appears to be typical of the frightened remnant in the midst of the Tribulation period. Jesus, Himself, warned that some future generation would need to flee to the mountains:

"When ye therefore shall see the abomination of desolation, spoken of by Daniel the prophet, stand in the holy place, (whoso readeth, let him understand:)
"Then let them which be in Judea flee into the mountains"
(Matthew 24:15,16).

The fleeing of Elijah into the wilderness appears to be a prophetic preview of that future remnant who will flee into the wilderness for safety. Furthermore, there were times during the ministry of Elijah when he was cared for by miracle provisions: first, when he was fed at the brook Cherith by the ravens; second, when the meal and the oil were multiplied in the widow's home; and third, when the angel fed him under the Juniper tree near Beersheba. Collectively, these events seem to represent God's provision for the Jewish remnant who will flee into the wilderness following the abomination of desolation.

After the brook Cherith dried up, Elijah went to the home of a widow who lived in Zarephath, a little town halfway between Tyre and Sidon. While he was there, he raised the widow's son from the dead. This could be a prophetic picture of the resurrection. There came a time when Elijah, himself, was translated into heaven. In a broad sense, it offers a prophetic picture of the rapture.

When Elijah fled into the wilderness of Sinai, he returned to the same mountain where Moses had received the Law. Like Moses, he stayed for forty days. At the end of those days there came a wind, an earthquake and a fire. These dramatic events appear to represent the natural disasters of the Tribulation period. After the wind, the earthquake and the fire, the still small voice of God said, *"What doest thou here, Elijah?"* (I Kings 19:13). The prophet began to complain. He claimed he was the only one who loved and served the Lord. To that, the Lord replied:

"Yet I have seven thousand in Israel, all the knees which have not bowed unto Baal, and every mouth which hath not kissed him" (I Kings 19:18).

The remnant was represented by the number 7,000. That number may be contrasted with a group of unbelievers found in the city of Jerusalem:

"And the same hour was there a great earthquake, and the tenth part of the city fell, and in the earthquake were slain of men seven thousand: and the remnant were affrighted, and gave glory to the God of heaven" (Revelation 11:13).

When the prophetic Moses and Elijah are raptured into heaven in the midst of the Tribulation Period, seven thousand men will be slain in an earthquake — a contrast to the seven thousand persecuted prophets during the ministry of Elijah. Isn't it amazing that every detail — even the earthquake — recorded from the life of Elijah will find its future fulfillment during the days of the Tribulation Period. In the opening chapter of II Kings, a group of fifty soldiers were sent to arrest Elijah:

"And Elijah answered and said to the captain of fifty, If I be a man of God, then let fire come down from heaven, and consume thee and thy fifty. And there came down fire from heaven, and consumed him and his fifty" (II Kings 1:10).

Elijah called fire down upon those who would arrest him. Prophetically, this represents the same kind of ability that will belong to the future Elijah:

"And if any man will hurt them, fire proceedeth out of their mouth, and devoureth their enemies: and if any man will hurt them, he must in this manner be killed" (Revelation 11:5).

Amazingly, over and over again, in one event after another, the life of Elijah seems to be a prophetic overview of those events predicted to occur when the prophet enters into his latter-day ministry.

Chapter Seventeen

You Are a Prophecy!

One of the most fascinating metaphors of God's plan of the ages can be seen in the life of every human being. Believe it or not, you are a prophecy! The life of the average person corresponds to the history of mankind. There is an uncanny relationship between the average 70-year lifespan of man and the estimated 7,000 years of world history which, according to the Bible, has been predetermined for the great human adventure. It is stranger than fiction. Each individual literally represents a microcosm of the collective human adventure — from Creation to the consummation.

Briefly, it could be described like this: A child is born — a picture of Creation. He grows up, gets a job, goes into business for himself, reaches the pinnacle of his career, and retires around the age of 60 to spend the next 10 years or so taking it easy —

enjoying the fruits of his labors, and letting his son take over the family business. Then he dies around the age of 70, moving on to a greater adventure.

Comparing retirement at the age of 60 to world history, the Bible teaches that the Son of God will come back to the earth at the end of 6,000 years to take over His Father's business while we enjoy a thousand years of rest — comparable to retirement.

Now let's go back to the beginning and get the details. We will see an uncanny relationship between the individual human adventure and the greater adventure for humanity as a whole.

The Dispensation of Innocence

Let us begin with the birth of a child. That can be compared to the dispensation of *Innocence* when Adam and Eve were created and placed in a beautiful garden under the watchful care of the heavenly Father. There is nothing quite so beautiful as a little baby. "Who does he look like?" "Well, he looks like Daddy," or, "He looks like Mommy." At least you have to admit he's been made in the image of his parents. In like manner, man was made in the image of God.

Ah, the newborn baby! — so innocent — placed in his own little Garden of Eden. So helpless, yet so perfect. But it doesn't take long for the little rascal to get into trouble. It's kind of hard to say just when that moment comes. But it doesn't take them long to learn that they can wrap you around their little finger just by crying in the middle of the night. The real test comes when the little darling pulls up to the coffee table and reaches for something he is not supposed to have. "No," you say, as you swat his cute little hand. That's when the little rascal is determined to have it in spite of all that you can do.

The Dispensation of Conscience

He is now removed from the dispensation of *Innocence* to enter the dispensation of *Conscience*. He has fallen and, oh, the guilt he feels! You can see it written across his face!

The Dispensation of Human Government

Suddenly, he finds himself under the discipline of the dispensation of *Human Government* — he falls under the despotic rule of father and mother. But it's for his own good. The child has to learn responsibility. "Adam, Eve, you must learn to till the soil. You must learn to eat by the sweat of your brow." "All right, Junior, make up your bed." "Wash your hands, Roger." The years come and go until the child is approaching the age of 10, and you can see that your little baby is growing up. He's losing his childishness. The Adam-image is fading away.

Adam died at the age of 930, slightly less than 1,000 years. In like manner, a child around the age of 9 or 10 begins to grow "like a weed" and lose his identity as the "baby of the family." Suddenly you realize you have a young man on your hands. The baby is gone.

The "Abel characteristic" can also be seen during those early years when a child loves freely and enjoys the delightfulness of his new adventure. He loves everybody. Even animals seem to take on an almost human characteristic — Bugs the Bunny, Donald the Duck, Teddy the Bear, and so on.

He hates no one and believes that everybody is good. Such was Abel, the son of Adam. But it doesn't take long in a young child's life for the likes of Cain to raise his ugly head. Thus develops the conflict between good and evil in the life of a child.

By the age of 13 the young teenager begins to face the problem of allegiance in his life. Until then he has owed his allegiance only to his father and mother. Now he begins to look around — to develop what we might call "idolatry." It may be simple like Superman or rebellious like Ringo Starr, but he has reached the age of idolatry.

Thus, it was — during the age of adolescent humanity when the world was 1,300 years old, 1,400, 1,500, etc. That was the age for the development of idolatry. When the world was 1,600 years old, the heavenly Father had to bring on a "flood" to wash away the ungodliness of the human race that He might preserve the righteous:

"... *every imagination of ... his heart* [is] *only evil continually*" (Genesis 6:5).

It is during those teenage years, somewhere around the age of 16, that a parent has to come to grips with the evil direction of his adolescent — so that he might be able to preserve and develop the good. Those are the "flood" years when evil is contemplated — perhaps even practiced — but, hopefully, purged.

During those years, every problem is overwhelming for the teenager. "My nose is too big! My ears stick out! My arms are too long! Nobody likes me." Every problem seems like a flood. But if the teenager will only try, he will find "grace" in the eyes of his father.

When he comes out of those years of turmoil, he will end up on the mountain top just like Noah — provided, of course, he stays in the safety of the family unit and doesn't jump out of the boat. It is during those flood years that the "Eden" environment of the home is washed away, and the teenager sees a new and unfriendly world awaiting him.

Just because he has found grace in the eyes of his father doesn't mean the teenager is now perfect, for those are the experimental years. For instance, one of the first things Noah did in his new world was to experiment with wine — and, oh, what a catastrophe it brought in his life! So it is with many young people today. Many begin to experiment with drugs — liquid or otherwise — which could have devastating results on their future.

Man is a trinity — made up of body, soul, and spirit, and during the teenage years, it is so easy for a young person to become enslaved to sin by yielding to its temptation. The "spirit" is that part of a man which becomes quite vulnerable during those years. Just as the curse was put upon Ham and his offspring causing them to become servants in the tents of his brethren; in like manner, the spirit can become enslaved to the body and its appetites.

Ham made light of his father's drunkenness and fell under a curse. In like manner, there are many young people who take sin far too lightly — and are in danger of becoming enslaved. It could put a mark upon one's character — comparable to that of Ham.

The Dispensation of Promise

Around the age of 20, a young man feels the need to leave home. "Go west, young man, go west. It's time to find your own promised land." That brings us near the age of 2,000 years in the great human adventure. God reached down to a man named Abraham and said:

"Get thee out of thy country, and from thy kindred, and from thy father's house, unto a land that I will show thee:
"And I will make of thee a great nation, and I will bless thee, and make thy name great; and thou shalt be a blessing" (Genesis 12:1,2).

"It's time to leave home. Leave your family and go west, young man, go west." The comparison is almost uncanny. When a young man leaves home, he does not become an overnight success in business. In like manner, Abraham did not immediately possess his Promised Land. He went to it and even lived in it, but he really didn't possess it. It wasn't his. It was there as a goal to be reached, but it remained only a "Promised" Land; it was not yet possessed.

So it is in the life of a young man. He may know what he wants to do, but the goal remains just beyond his grasp. He is going to have to attend the "university of hard knocks" before he can obtain his goal. Thus, we enter upon the dispensation of *Promise*, which lasted in human history from Abraham to Moses.

During the years from 20 to 25, a young man is tempted to live a pretty worldly life. He may rebel against those around him as the sons of Jacob rebelled against Joseph — and eventually may end up in the proverbial "Egyptian bondage!"

The Dispensation of Law

At the age of 2,500 years, mankind entered into a new dispensation which was to last for the next 1,500 years. It is called the dispensation of *Law*. In like manner, around the age of 25, a young man begins to settle down in life. He establishes some basic moral values — comparable to the Ten Commandments. This is when he realizes that if he is going to get anywhere in life, he is going to have to go to work. The college student can no longer play around. He has to get down to business. The "hippie" finally puts on a suit and tie and joins the real world.

It is also around the age of 25 when a young man finds the girl of his choice and marries her. Thus, the dispensation of *Law* begins. God the Father in heaven reached down and pulled the girl of His dreams out of Egyptian bondage and married her, for, you see, the Chosen People became "the wife" of Jehovah.

There was a covenant established between Jehovah and Israel when the human race was 2,500 years old and in like manner, a groom and his bride establish a marriage covenant.

Many young men between the ages of 20 and 25 find themselves in a proverbial Egyptian bondage. But the wise young man makes his exodus and wanders for a while through the wilderness of this life while he establishes his covenant with a "chosen" person — the girl of his dreams and establishes some moral concepts which will govern him for the rest of his life.

For the next 15 years (between the ages of 25 and 40) those moral concepts are definitely "law." They are engraved, so to speak, on "tablets of stone." They are not yet made a part of the personality. But a man follows them — his wife will see to that!

Those are the years when a man produces his firstborn son. We can see that in the great human adventure as God told Moses to deliver a message to Pharaoh, *"Israel is My son, even My firstborn"* (Exodus 4:22). And so, around the age of 25, a man produces his firstborn son, and the cycle seems to start all over again — except from a different perspective. He who once viewed life through the eyes of a son, now sees life from the viewpoint of a father.

For the next five years or so (from 25 to 30) a man may conquer his "promised land." But it is a struggle. During those years, it is hard to get a business loan from the bank. Few bankers are willing to make a big loan until the client reaches the age of 30. Oh, he may be able to finance an automobile or even a house, but there aren't very many people in their twenties who can borrow $50,000 or $100,000 for a business venture.

Around the age of 30 a man becomes mature and wise, like Solomon who appeared on the stage of human history after 3,000 years. This is the time when the "Solomon characteristic" is developed — a time of wisdom and maturity.

Also, it was a time when Solomon built the house of God. So it is in the life of a man around the age of 30 when he gets his children in Sunday school and church, for he wants that little four, five, or six year old to learn the Bible. He doesn't want his child making the same mistakes he made.

For the next few years (between the ages of 30 and 40) a man will reach a measure of success, but will see some failures, as well. Sometimes, during those years a man's kingdom may be divided — as it was in Israel after the death of Solomon. It may be that a man will experience an "Assyrian" captivity and never recover — or a "Babylonian" captivity that will only last a little while.

Around the 3,300 year point the northern tribes went into Assyrian captivity, and 100 years later the southern tribes went into Babylonian captivity. So it is in the life of a man in his mid-30's. If his kingdom is divided, he is going to be under a lot of pressure.

He might make a few bad decisions. Not all business decisions will be good ones. He is going to have to suffer some financial captivities. Hopefully, they won't last long, and at least a part of him recovers. The Babylonian captivity only lasted 70 years, and God's people came back to rebuild their homeland.

The Dispensation of Grace

Around the age of 40, a man reaches a turning point in his life. It either becomes a "mid-life crisis" — or we might say that "life begins at 40." It all depends on how a man copes with those special problems unique to that time in his life. That brings us to the 4,000 year point in world history. The choice was to either reject the Messiah and compound the problems of life or receive Him and enjoy the glories of the kingdom.

Which shall it be? At 40, a man has been married somewhere between 15 to 20 years (give or take a few). His firstborn son has reached the age of adolescence. The father expects a lot out of his son — just like Israel was expecting of their messiah. But when Jesus came, He didn't seem to measure up to Israel's concept of a Savior. They wanted a messiah who could overthrow the Roman government and set up the kingdom.

But at that point in history, Jesus had come for quite another reason. He came looking for a bride of His own — New Testament Gentile Christianity. And in like manner, a young man at that stage in life begins looking for the girl of his dreams — his own chosen person. Furthermore, when a son becomes a teen-ager, his dad wants him to be about the father's business. Perhaps he enters as an apprentice — preparing for that day when he will become a full partner, but the young messiah doesn't quite measure up to expectations, and there are some things is his life the father would like to crucify. For the son it may be a flood experience, but for the father, it is a crucifixion. Besides, the father doesn't want that young whippersnapper running things around his household. He'll not have the son rule over him!

From a business viewpoint, those are the greatest years of opportunity in a man's life. He reaches the top of his career between the ages of 40 and 60. The potential is unlimited. If a man has not found himself to be successful by the age of 40, he usually changes his direction. At least he opens his vision — and his business begins to spread out. Some men turn their local business into a nationwide chain, and for some — the scope may be worldwide. That's what the Father did 2,000 years ago. He expanded His work of redemption and made the Gospel available on a worldwide scale. He took the Gospel to the ends of the earth. It became like an international franchise.

The years between 40 and 60 represent the dispensation of *Grace*. That's when the dispensation of *Law*, which began around the age of 25, turns into *"Grace"* around 40. A man's "heart of stone" finally becomes a "heart of flesh." It is when a man no longer has to make himself do what is right. It finally becomes an automatic part of a man's character.

The Dispensation of Rest

When a man reaches the age of 60, it's time to retire. It's time to turn the family business over to the son and let him have it on his own — while the old man sits back and relaxes to enjoy the next 10 years of his life, for he has worked enough. He should be able to enjoy the "fruits of his labor." So it is in the great worldwide human adventure. This is the time when the dispensation of *Grace* will turn into the dispensation of *Rest*.

The kingdom has come. Remember, when you were a baby, you lived under the dispensation of *Innocence*. But then you learned "right from wrong" and fell under the dispensation of *Conscience*. During those years you found yourself under the dispensation of *Human Government* — the rule of father and mother. But around the age of 20 you entered upon the dispensation of *Promise*, looking forward to a bright future. However, somewhere between 20 and 25 you ended up in a proverbial "Egyptian" bondage. But you didn't stay. You made your exodus out of that volatile life-style to settle down and enter upon the dispensation of *Law*. You got married and established some guidelines for life. But by the age of 40, you entered the dispensation of *Grace*. The things you did, you wanted to do. And at the age of 60 you entered upon the seventh dispensation of your life, the *Kingdom Rest*, when you turned the family business over to your son.

It all represents a prophecy of 7,000 years for the great human adventure. Today, this old world is nearing the age of 60 — or perhaps we should say 6,000. It's almost time to turn the family business over to the heavenly Father's Son and retire. That is why I sincerely believe Jesus Christ will soon make His appearance to take over the Father's business. He will establish the golden age of world history. Say, I wonder if that's why we call those years after 60 the golden years? I believe they are going to be wonderful years. Christ (the Son) will rule and reign as King of kings and Lord of lords. My, how successful He is going to be! He's going to conquer the problems of a wayward world.

The last enemy to be conquered is death. For you see, at 70 a man leaves this old house of clay and enters upon a new and eternal adventure. Likewise, at the age of 7,000 this old world is going to be renovated. God will make *"new heavens and a new earth wherein dwelleth righteousness"* (II Peter 3:13).

So there you have it. The parallels are uncanny. They could not possibly be coincidental. It is obvious to see the grand design — 70 years for the individual human adventure and 7,000 years for the great worldwide human adventure. God declared His ancient plan in the life of every man.